GLADSTONE *and* DISRAELI

Michael Lynch

008 180

D0493488

Hodder & Stoughton
LONDON SYDNEY AUCKLAND TORONTO

ACKNOWLEDGEMENTS

The publishers wish to thank the following for their permission to reproduce copyright illustrations:

The Governing Body, Christ Church, Oxford: cover (Gladstone); The Hulton Picture Company: p96; The Illustrated London News Picture Library: p92; The Mansell Collection: pp13, 40, 54, 67, 108; The Mary Evans Picture Library: p21; National Portrait Gallery: cover (Disraeli); Reproduced by permission of *Punch*: p33.

The publishers would like to thank the following for permission to reproduce material in this volume:

Edward Arnold for the extract from *Conservatism and the Conservative Party in the Nineteenth Century* by B. Coleman (1988); Longman Group UK for the extract from *Gladstone, Disraeli and later Victorian Politics* by Paul Adelman (1970); Macmillan Ltd for the extracts from *Gladstone as Politician* by Agatha Ramm and *Religion: A Collection of Founder's Day Lectures delivered at St Deniol's Library, Hawarden* by Lord Blake, ed. Peter J. Jagger (1985); Methuen, London for the extracts from *Disraeli* by Robert Blake (1966); Oxford University Press for the extracts from *Gladstone 1809–74* by HCG Matthew (1988); Routledge for the extract from *Disraeli* by John K. Walton (1990).

Every effort has been made to trace and acknowledge ownership of copyright.

The publishers will be glad to make suitable arrangements with any copyright holders whom it has not been possible to contact.

British Library Cataloguing in Publication Data
Lynch, Michael
  Gladstone and Disraeli. – (History at source)
  I. Title II. Series
  941.081

ISBN 0–340–54826–6

First published 1991

© 1991 Michael J Lynch

All rights reserved. No part of this publication may be reproduced or transmitted in any form or by any means, electronic or mechanical, including photocopy, recording, or any information storage and retrieval system, without permission in writing from the publisher or under licence from the Copyright Licensing Agency Limited. Further details of such licences (for reprographic reproduction) may be obtained from the Copyright Licensing Agency Limited of 33–34 Alfred Place, London WC1E 7DP.

Printed in Great Britain for the educational publishing division of Hodder & Stoughton Ltd, Mill Road, Dunton Green, Sevenoaks, Kent by Page Bros Ltd, Norwich

CONTENTS

APPROACHING SOURCE-BASED
QUESTIONS

The aims of this book are to provide a set of key documents illustrating the careers of Gladstone and Disraeli and to suggest, by a series of questions and sample answers, how the source material can best be analysed and interpreted.

With the adoption by the examination boards of a common core syllabus, questions based on documents and sources now form a compulsory part of their papers. Many boards include such questions in their outline courses and all make source-material questions a dominant feature of their depth studies. In this latter type of paper, it is usual for as much as 50 per cent of the total marks to be allocated to the document section. There is a variation in the type of question set. Some boards require candidates to study prescribed texts, extracts from which appear on the examination paper for analysis. Other boards suggest a wider range of source material for study without indicating specific texts; detailed questions are then set on document extracts which will not necessarily have been seen previously, but which candidates should be able to analyse by reference to their knowledge of the course.

It is important that candidates appreciate the weighting that the examination boards now give to the documentary approach in the study of History. There is a broad measure of agreement between the boards with regard to the integral place that document study now has in the common core syllabuses.

This work gives a range of different types of source-based questions. Some examination questions are essentially a comprehension exercise, testing the candidate's ability to read and understand a historical document. Other questions examine candidates' background knowledge of wider themes or probe their understanding of special topics. The most demanding questions are those which ask for an assessment of the historical value of a given document or for a comparative evaluation of separate sources.

All examination papers indicate the number of marks on offer for each question, the practice followed in this book. These are important as a clear guide to the relative importance of the question in the overall examination paper and show what proportion of the candidate's time should be spent on each question. It is not unusual for poorer examinees to write at essay length on parts of questions that carry only one mark! As a rule of thumb, it is worth bearing in mind that for each mark offered there should be a corresponding point of fact or analysis; this is a broad, working guide and should not be followed slavishly. It is not suggested that candidates waste valuable time and effort trying to find an artificial extra point of their own merely to satisfy an apparent numerical requirement.

Care should be taken, as with full essay answers, to deal with the question as set. An examinee asked to evaluate the significance of a document will gain little simply from paraphrasing it or giving irrelevant details about its background. As well as showing understanding of sources, candidates are expected, at this level, to have an appreciation of historiography; that is, to know something about the problems involved in writing history. Questions are now frequently set which require the candidate's ability to spot bias, attitude and motive in the writer of a given extract. The specimen answers in this book are intended to help in this regard, but certain general pointers are worth mentioning here. When faced with questions about possible bias in a source, candidates should pose themselves such queries as: Is the writer of the extract evidently angry, bitter, confident, detached, involved? Is the document an official report or a personal reminiscence? Does the passage suggest that it is being written for a particular audience or is it a general statement? Is it propaganda or objective reporting? If candidates train themselves to respond in this way to the sources that they meet in their course study, they will develop the type of observational and analytical skills that merit high marks when appropriately used in examinations.

Another consideration, of no small account to examinees, is that a good grounding in document-based work, by broadening their knowledge and sharpening their appreciation of historical material, will prove of inestimable benefit in their handling of full essays. The virtues of this 'knock-on' effect are very apparent to the examiners, as witness this comment from one of their reports: 'It is most unlikely that the highest grades will be awarded to candidates who do not show an awareness of the importance of first sources and an ability to quote relevantly from them.'

INTRODUCTION

British politics in the nineteenth century was dominated by three outstanding party leaders and premiers: Robert Peel, Benjamin Disraeli and William Gladstone. All three men began their lives as Tories, but each dramatically diverged from the political path on which he had set out. Indeed, it is possible to argue, as many of their contemporary critics did, that each of them betrayed the party to which he had first belonged. Peel turned the Tory Party into the Conservative Party, but only through accepting changes (Catholic Emancipation in 1829, the Great Reform Act of 1832, and the repeal of the Corn laws in 1846) that were a direct rejection of previous Tory principles. Disraeli chose to make his reputation as a young politician by attacking Peel, his leader. Such attacks played a part in the defeat of Peel over Corn Law repeal in 1846 and the consequent split of the Conservative Party. Gladstone was Peel's protégé but he abandoned his Tory roots to join the Liberal Party in the 1850s (Chapter 1).

In some respects Disraeli and Gladstone were unrepresentative of their parties. As a Jew of modest social background, lacking the traditional public school, Oxford or Cambridge, education, Disraeli was regarded by many Conservatives as an upstart. The only reason that they eventually accepted such an unlikely figure as their leader was that they simply could not do without him. In the words of his principal modern biographer, Robert Blake, Disraeli's political skills and experience made him 'an indispensable liability' to the Conservative Party (Chapter 4). Gladstone's Liberalism was more an expression of his own personal attitudes and ideas than a workable set of party-political principles. Despite being the dominant Liberal statesman of his time, he paid little attention to the details of party organisation and was quite prepared to subordinate the interests of the Liberal Party to what he regarded as higher causes. It is arguable that the decline of the Liberals in the twentieth century was directly linked to Gladstone's failure to adjust his Party's policies to meet the changing economic and social circumstances of late Victorian Britain (Chapter 5).

As a young politician Disraeli deliberately exploited his distinctive Jewish appearance and outrageous style of dress to make himself known. He calculated that effective self-publicity would help off-set the disadvantage of not belonging to the social class from which politicians were traditionally drawn. His tactics sometimes invited ridicule, but there was no doubting he was a person of exceptional talent. He became a leading member of Young England, a movement which looked to a romantic, golden, English past which was to be restored under the leadership of the aristocracy. Although the English aristocracy remained a matter of life-long fascination for Disraeli, it is unlikely that he ever took the ideas of Young England very seriously. The movement was a means of promoting himself and it provided a platform from which to attack Peel. In the 1840s Disraeli came to prominence with the ferocity of his onslaught on Peel for his betrayal of traditional Conservative values in contemplating the repeal of the Corn Laws (Chapter 1).

However, the striking point about Disraeli's subsequent career is that in all major respects he remained a Peelite. After he had 'climbed to the top of the greasy pole' and become the Conservative leader and Prime Minister in the late 1860s, he followed policies which were essentially developments of what Peel had begun earlier. The acceptance of free trade and of parliamentary reform are the major examples of this. It was once said of Disraeli that, just as a sculptor perceives his finished creation in the untouched block of rough marble, so he perceived the importance of the working-class voter in future English politics. Modern scholars tend to think of this as exaggeration; they see Disraeli's appreciation of the need to enfranchise the working class as a question of opportunism rather than perception (Chapter 2).

Of greater significance for the development of the Conservative Party was Disraeli's major achievement in winning over large sections of the middle class. Notwithstanding his admiration for aristocratic tradition, he understood that it was the middle class who mattered. They were the possessors of the wealth created by the industrial revolution. Now that they possessed the vote, they were the most influential stratum in politics and society. No party could survive if it did not adapt itself to this fundamental social and economic shift. The struggle that this entailed was evident in the dramatic parliamentary confrontations between Disraeli and Gladstone after 1868. It was in that year that Gladstone's great Liberal reforming Ministry began. Between 1868 and 1874 hardly any major institution was left untouched (Chapter 3). Seizing the opportunity to portray Gladstone as a crazed destroyer of the country's good, Disraeli mounted a successful campaign to present Conservatism as a rational, progressive alternative. In the early 1870s Disraeli redefined his Party as a force concerned to maintain traditional national values and institutions but not unwilling to consider moderate reform (Chapter 4). It was in this period that he began to make imperialism an essential feature of Conservatism (Chapter 6).

The reward for his efforts came in 1874 with a defeat of Gladstone at the polls. In power from that date until 1880, Disraeli embarked on a series of social and administrative reforms that were no less significant than those of the previous Liberal Government.

However, it was not over domestic affairs but foreign policy that the last great contest between the two adversaries was fought. Disraeli's support for Turkey against Russia in the Eastern Question was interpreted by Gladstone as condoning Turkish atrocities against her subject peoples. The fierce exchanges between the two British statesmen over this represented a deep divide in the nation at large (Chapter 9). The dispute did not prevent Disraeli (Lord Beaconsfield from 1876) from achieving his greatest diplomatic victory. At the Congress of Berlin in 1878, his was the outstanding personality. The terms of the Treaty that was signed there, with its restrictions on Russian expansion, reflected the influence he had exerted (Chapter 8).

Important though the differences between the policies of Disraeli and Gladstone were, the major distinction between them was not one of politics but of personality. The two men could hardly have been more dissimiliar in temperament and character. There was little humour in Gladstone. There was much in Disraeli; he once observed that the reason why he was not universally popular in England was that he was never 'grave' enough for English taste (Chapter 10).

Lack of gravity was not a charge that could ever be laid agaist Gladstone. He was, from the first, a person of the utmost seriousness. Deeply religious, he kept a daily diary throughout his life, his 'account book with God', as M R D Foot, the first editor of the published *Gladstone Diaries*, describes it. In his youth, Gladstone seriously considered taking holy orders, and, even after he had turned to politics, he still saw his public life as essentially a matter of serving God. He was remarkably reactionary as a young Tory politician. He was appalled by the Great Reform Act of 1832 and by the Whig reforms of the 1830s, particularly those concerning the Established Church. It was his intense admiration for Robert Peel, under whom he served as a junior minister in the 1834–5 and 1841–6 Governments, that began to modify some of his harsher views, but it has to be said that, despite his great intellectual gifts, Gladstone was often confused in his political thinking during this period. This explains the uncertainty of his position following the split in the Conservative Party in 1846. Although an obvious Peelite in terms of his veneration for Peel's memory, Gladstone made no consistent effort to rebuild a Conservative-Peelite party (Chapter 1).

It was as Chancellor of the Exchequer, first in Aberdeen's Coalition (1852–5), and then in Palmerston's Government (1859–65), that Gladstone made his first great mark on English politics. His acceptance of office under Palmerston, a man for whom he had previously had as deep a distaste as for Disraeli, was a clear sign that he was no longer a Peelite in any sense that mattered. From 1859 onwards Gladstone could be counted as a Liberal.

Within another decade he had become leader of that Party. In 1868, by then in his sixtieth year, he became Prime Minister for the first time. During the next six years Gladstone headed one of the outstanding reforming ministries in parliamentary history. This 'high tide of Liberalism' produced a range of legislation affecting the law, the Civil

Service, Ireland, the universities, the Army, education, and the Church (Chapter 3). So extensive was the range of the reforms that considerable opposition was aroused among the vested interests affected. The result was a heavy defeat for Gladstone and the Liberals in the election of 1874. Characteristically, Gladstone spoke of his Government's having been 'borne down on a torrent of gin and beer', a reference to the brewers' campaign against him in revenge for the Liberals' tightening of the licensing laws.

Following this defeat, Gladstone resigned as premier and as leader of the Liberal Party. His declared intention was to withdraw from politics in order to prepare himself to meet his maker. However, in 1876 he was brought out of retirement by the Turkish atrocities, on which he felt compelled to speak. Gladstone made a telling contribution to the national debate on the Eastern Question by publishing his pamphlet, '*The Bulgarian Horrors and the Question of the East*', an anti-Turkish blast that polarised English attitudes (Chapter 9). Gladstone had now developed a belief in the basic goodness and moral sense of the British people, which, he considered, transcended class differences, as was evident in their response to the Bulgarian horrors. He said he would always 'back the masses against the classes'.

In 1879, his brilliant campaign in the Midlothian constituency, denouncing the evils of 'Beaconsfieldism', made him again the indisputable leader of the Liberals, though this had not been his original intention (Chapter 5). Returned to office in 1880 as Prime Minister for the second time, Gladstone was beset by difficulties. Contrary to his own anti-imperialism, he found himself drawn into authorising the British occupation of Egypt in 1882, a decision that caused a crisis of conscience in the Liberal Party and began a foreign involvement that brought considerable embarrassment to the Government. Gladstone incurred widespread condemnation when his refusal to send a relief force to the Sudan appeared to have occasioned the death there, in 1885, of the national hero, General Gordon.

Above all, it was Ireland that pressed upon the Liberal leader. He sought again to fulfil the promise he had first made in 1868, that he would 'pacify Ireland'. Ireland was, indeed, to dominate the rest of his political life. In 1885 Gladstone came to his momentous decision that Home Rule was unavoidable if the Irish Question was to be settled. His conversion, which let the Conservative Party off the Home Rule hook by committing the Liberals to it, changed the course of English politics. Gladstone's perseverance in bringing in Irish Home Rule Bills in 1886 and 1893, in the face of opposition from the Conservatives, the House of Lords, and half his own Party, was an act of impressive personal courage, but it split the Liberal Party and allowed the Unionists to dominate English politics for twenty years (Chapter 7).

Gladstone was more than simply a prime minister and party leader;

he became a moral force in English public life. The outstanding figure of his time, he had a profound, though not necessarily a progressive, effect on the development of English politics. As his successful arousing of public opinion over the Turkish atrocities and in the Midlothian Campaign indicated, Gladstone was able to identify himself as 'the people's William', yet in most respects his own interests and attitudes detached him from the ordinary concerns of politics. Two crusades consumed his time and overshadowed his politics from the 1870s onwards – the Eastern Question and Ireland. Magnificent though he was in fighting for these great causes, his pre-occupation with them obliged him to neglect issues which many of his fellow Liberals regarded as more pressing.

It was at this critical time, that the Liberal Party faced a crisis of identity; what in an increasingly industrialised and democratic age did Liberalism represent? For the traditional Whigs within the Party, the answer was the preservation of the character and constitution of England, objectives little different from traditional Conservatism. For the radicals, the answer was that the Liberal Party should be embracing the social problems of the day: poverty, ill-health and urban squalor. Joseph Chamberlain, the foremost radical in the Party and a potential Liberal leader, viewed Gladstone's obsession with Ireland as a distraction from these vital concerns. The Whigs and radicals were struggling for the soul of the Liberal Party, a struggle which Gladstone seemed unable or unwilling to recognise (Chapter 10).

The problem was intensified by Gladstone's reluctance to retire. So long as he remained in politics, no one could seriously challenge him for the leadership of the Liberal Party. His disinclination to withdraw frustrated the younger contenders for Liberal Party leadership. This was more than a check on the ambitions of such as Chamberlain; it meant that, for as long as Gladstone remained, the Liberal Party was essentially *his* party. It could not become primarily a party of policies. By the time he did finally retire in 1894 it was too late; the Party had split. Most Whigs had become Liberal-Unionists, indistinguishable from the Conservatives; most radicals had despaired of the Party's becoming socially relevant, a claim they proved by pointing to the failure of Liberalism to win sufficient support from the growing ranks of organised labour (Chapter 5).

Gladstone's own perception of his crusading role led to his leaving the critical matter of his Party's development unattended. The Liberal Party, with its problems unresolved and its character undecided, entered the twentieth century ill-equipped for the tasks it was obliged to undertake. In this respect, extraordinary though Gladstone's career had been in the degree of domination that it exercised over its times, it was in a party-political sense a negative one. Gladstonian Liberalism died with Gladstone (Chapter 10).

Outline of Gladstone's Career

1809	born in Liverpool, into a prosperous merchant family of Scottish extraction
1821–7	attends Eton College
1828–31	at Oxford University
1831	speaks in the Oxford Union against the Reform Bill
1832	enters parliament as a Tory MP for Newark
1835	appointed Colonial Secretary in Peel's Government (1834–5)
1838	his first book, *The State in its Relations with the Church*, is published
1839	marries Catherine Glynne
1843	enters Peel's Government (1841–6) as President of the Board of Trade
1844	introduces Railway Act
1845	resigns from Cabinet over the Maynooth grant
1847	elected MP for Oxford University
1848	serves as special constable during the Chartist demonstration
1850–1	visits Naples and speaks out against Neapolitan tyranny
1852	appointed Chancellor of the Exchequer in Aberdeen's Whig-Peelite Government (1852–5)
1853	introduces his first Budget
1855	declines to continue as Chancellor of the Exchequer under Palmerston
1859	agrees to join Palmerston's Whig-Liberal Government (1859–65) as Chancellor of the Exchequer
1862	supports the Confederacy in the American Civil War
1865	defeated at Oxford – elected for South Lancashire
1867	opposes Disraeli's Reform Bill
1868	becomes leader of the Liberal Party
	Prime Minister for the first time after inflicting electoral defeat on Disraeli and the Conservatives
1868–74	leads great reforming Liberal government
1874	resigns as PM
1875	gives up his leadership of the Liberal Party and announces his retirement from politics
1876	is brought out of retirement by the Turkish atrocities; makes a national impact with his pamphlet, *The Bulgarian Horrors and the Question of the East*
1879	undertakes his celebrated Midlothian Campaign; his success makes his resumption of Liberal leadership unavoidable
1880	becomes PM for the second time following a major electoral victory over 'Beaconsfieldism'
1880–5	his second ministry is largely concerned with Ireland, parliamentary reform and foreign affairs – the question of Egypt

1885	Gladstone resigns as PM; his conversion to Irish Home Rule becomes publicly known
1886	becomes PM for the third time; introduces the first Irish Home Rule Bill; this is defeated and his Party is split
1892	becomes PM for the fourth time
1892–4	his fourth ministry is pre-occupied with Ireland
1893	introduces the second Irish Home Rule Bill; this passes in the Commons but is defeated in the Lords
1894	resigns as PM and finally retires from politics
1898	dies

Outline of Disraeli's Career

1804	born in London into a Jewish family of comfortable private means
1814–21	attends little-known schools in Blackheath and Epping Forest
1817	becomes a Christian
1821	articled to a firm of solicitors
1826	his first novel, *Vivian Grey*, is published
1826–32	goes on a grand tour of Europe
1832	stands for parliament but is defeated at High Wycombe
1837	enters parliament as Conservative MP for Maidstone; makes disastrous maiden speech in the House of Commons
1839	marries Mrs Mary Wyndham Lewis
1841–6	becomes a leading figure in the Young England movement
1844–7	his three major novels, *Coningsby*, *Sybil* and *Tancred*, published
1845–6	leads a campaign against Peel over repeal of the Corn Laws
1852	becomes Chancellor of the Exchequer in Derby's Government
1858–9	again Chancellor of Exchequer in Derby's second Government
1866–7	outmanoeuvres Gladstone and the Liberals and pushes through the Second Reform Bill (1867)
1868	becomes PM for the first time, but is defeated in the general election
1868–74	exploits the growing unpopularity of Gladstone to rejuvenate the Conservative Party
1872	makes a series of key speeches redefining the role of the Conservative Party
1874	wins general election and becomes PM for the second time
1874–80	leads one of the great reforming ministries of the century
1876	is raised to the peerage as Lord Beaconsfield
1878	makes a major impact on international affairs at the Congress of Berlin
1880	Conservatives defeated in the general election
1881	dies

1 GLADSTONE AND DISRAELI – THEIR EARLY CAREERS

Gladstone was born into a prosperous middle-class family. As a young man, he was intensely religious and serious. At Eton and Oxford he showed himself to be a first-class scholar. He first contemplated entering the church as a career, but eventually decided that he could best fulfil his religious duties by serving God in public life. In his early years in politics Gladstone was very much a reactionary. He was a bitter opponent of the 1832 Reform Act and the Whig measures of the 1830s, particularly their Church Reforms [A-D].

Gladstone and Disraeli were both highly romantic young men, but Gladstone lacked the charm and ease of manner that characterised Disraeli. As well as becoming outstanding politicians, they each established a reputation as a writer, Gladstone of heavy theology and political analysis, Disraeli of political and romantic novels [E,F,H].

Disraeli's background made him an outsider in English politics. With the exception of the Duke of Wellington, he was the only Prime Minister in the nineteenth century not to have attended public school and either Oxford or Cambridge University, the traditional training grounds of British politicians. As his family had formally become Anglicans, Disraeli's Jewishness was not a direct barrier to his political progress, but it was one of the factors that led to his being regarded as something of an upstart. Disraeli deliberately cultivated a high-profile style of appearance in order to make himself known [I-L].

In the early 1840s Disraeli became the unofficial leader of a movement within the Conservative Party known as 'Young England'. This was a group of Tories who believed in a return to rule by the aristocracy. In looking back to a mythical past, they were reacting against the 1832 Reform Act and the bureaucratic, utilitarian reforms, that followed it. They held the romantic notion that, loyal to the traditions of England, a benevolent aristocracy could lead the working classes in recreating a new 'Young England', based on the principles that had formerly made the nation great. It is doubtful that Disraeli ever took these ideas seriously, but he found 'Young England' useful to him personally. It provided him with something of a power base in Parliament and the party, and it enabled him to promote his own personal position by means of a series of attacks on Peel's leadership. The culmination of his vendetta came with his condemnation of Peel's 1846 repeal of the corn laws, the measure that split the Conservatives and led to the emergence during the following twenty years of the newly-formed Conservative and Liberal Parties [M-Q].

Disraeli's appointment as Chancellor of the Exchequer in 1852 marked an important stage on his path to leadership of the Conservative Party. However, it was the difficulties that Disraeli encountered as Chancellor that provided Gladstone with the opportunity to take over that position himself. Gladstone's achievements in financial planning, advanced in a series of brilliant budgets in the 1850s and 60s, consolidated his reputation as a public figure. In 1859 Gladstone at last swallowed his personal objections to Palmerston and joined the Liberals. The death of Palmerston in 1865 left Gladstone the dominant figure in the party. Three years later he became Prime Minister of a Liberal Government [R-T].

A Gladstone discusses his choice of career with his father

If I advert to the disposition of my own mind . . . I cannot avoid perceiving that it has inclined to the ministerial office [holy orders]. My mind involuntarily reverts to the sad and solemn conviction that a fearfully great portion of the world round me is dying in sin . . . how, my beloved parent, can I bear to think of my own seeking to wanton in the pleasures of life (I mean even its innocent pleasures), or give up my heart to its business, while my fellow-creatures, to whom I am bound by every tie of human sympathies, of a common sinfulness and a common redemption, day after day are sinking into death? I mean, not the death of the body, which is a gate either to happiness or to misery, but that of the soul, the true and the only true death. Can I, with this persuasion engrossing me, be justified in inactivity? or in any measure short of the most direct and effective means of meeting, if in *any degree* it be possible, these horrible calamities. Of my duties *to men* as a social being, can any be so important as to tell them of the danger under which I believe them to lie. . .

Gladstone to his father, 4 August 1830

B Gladstone's father points him towards a public career

You know my opinion to be, that the field for actual usefulness to our fellow-creatures . . . is more circumscribed and limited in the occupations and duties of a clergyman, whose sphere of action . . . is necessarily confined to his parish, than in those professions or pursuits which lead to a more general knowledge, as well as a more general intercourse with mankind. . . You are young and have ample time before you. Let nothing be done rashly; be consistent with yourself, and avail yourself of all the advantages within your reach.

John Gladstone to his son, 10 August 1830

C In old age Gladstone describes his reactionary youth

I think I must have had at this time [the 1830s] coming upon me some dread of a developed Liberalism as a rebellion against God and as a foe to Christianity. . .

I remember some foolish pranks: such, for example, as printing at my own costs and charges some foolish anti-reform placards based upon the idea, then standing for gospel with anti-reformers, that simply and without qualification reform was revolution.

from *My Earlier Political Opinions* (July 1892)

D Gladstone's Anti-Reform Handbill of 1831

People of England!

You are called on to exercise your suffrages in favour of men who wish to establish a NEW CONSTITUTION.

Before you vote, ask yourselves the following question, and let no man

DIVERT YOUR ATTENTION FROM THEM.

1 What has *South America* gained by new constitutions? Confusion.
2 What has *France* gained by a new constitution? Disorganisation.
3 What has *Belgium* gained by a new constitution? Starvation.
4 What is *'Old England'* to gain by a new constitution? and
5 What am *I* to gain by a new constitution?

Answer these for yourselves: vote for men who are solemnly pledged:

1 To redress every grievance.
2 To remove every blemish.
3 TO RESIST REVOLUTION TO THE DEATH.

E Disraeli woos Mary Wyndham Lewis

I cannot reconcile Love and separation. My ideas of Love are the perpetual enjoyment of the society of the sweet being to whom I am devoted, the sharing of every thought and even every fancy, of every charm and every care. Perhaps I sigh for a state which never can be mine, which never existed. But there is nothing in my own heart that convinces me it is impossible, and if it be an illusion it is an illusion worthy of the gods. I wish to be with you, to live with you, never to be away from you – I care not where, in heaven or on earth or in the waters under the earth.

Disraeli to Mary Wyndham Lewis, October 1838

F Gladstone woos Catherine Glynne

I address you, my dear Miss Glynne, in terms below my desires, yet perhaps beyond my right to say in the simple words which I believe

G Gladstone and Disraeli as young politicians

will in any event be most acceptable to you, and which no occasion has offered to address to you otherwise than by letter. My heart and hand are at your disposal.

I seek much in a wife in gifts better than those of our human pride, and am also sensible that she can find little in me; sensible that, were you to treat this note as the offspring of utter presumption, I must not be surprised; sensible that the lot I invite you to share, even if it be not attended, as I trust it is not, with peculiar disdvantages of an outward kind, is one, I do not say unequal to your deserts, for that were saying little, but liable at best to changes and perplexities and pains which, for myself, I contemplate without apprehension, but to which it is perhaps selfishness in the main, with the sense of inward dependence counteracting an opposite sense of my too real unworthiness, which would make me contribute to expose another – and that other!

With esteem, with gratitude, suffer me by one more act of boldness to add, with warm and true affection,

I am, Yours,
W E Gladstone

Gladstone to Catherine Glynne, 17 January 1839

H Gladstone reflects on the first night of his honeymoon

... the beloved sleeps for a while on the sofa – we have read the two second lessons [of the Prayer Book] together.

She has *less* cause to rejoice as well as more to weep; but with me this joy is not tempered enough, I fear & hardly belongs to a follower of the Crucified, much less to one so false in his profession. It has been more of heaven than of earth today. Life cannot yield such another sight...

She sleeps gently as a babe. O may I never disturb her precious peace, but cherish her more dearly than myself in proportion as she is less earthly.

from the entry for 25 July 1839 in *The Gladstone Diaries*

I A description of Disraeli's public style in 1835

He commenced in a lisping, lackadaisical tone of voice... He minced his phrases in apparently the most affected manner, and, whilst he was speaking, placed his hands in all imaginable positions; not because he felt awkward, and did not know, like a booby in a drawing-room, where to put them, but apparently for the purpose of exhibiting to the best advantage the glittering rings which decked his white and taper fingers. Now he would place his thumbs in the armholes of his waistcoat, and spread out his fingers on its flashing surface; then one set of digits would be released and he would lean affectedly on the table, supporting himself with his right hand; anon he would push aside the curls from his forehead... But as he proceeded all traces of this dandyism and affectation were lost. With a rapidity of utterance perfectly astonishing he referred to past events and indulged in anticipations of the future. In all he said he proved himself to be the finished orator – every period was rounded with the utmost elegance, and in his most daring flights, when one trembled lest he should fall from the giddy height to which he had attained, he so gracefully descended that every hearer was wrapt in admiring surprise... His voice, at first so finical, gradually became full, musical, and sonorous, and with every varying sentient was beautifully modulated. His arms no longer appeared to be exhibited for show, but he exemplified the eloquence of the hand. The dandy was transformed ... into a practised orator and finished elocutionist.

Dorset County Chronicle, 30 April 1835

J Disraeli's maiden speech in parliament in 1837 was greeted with ridicule.

When we remember at the same time that, with emancipated Ireland and enslaved England, on the one hand a triumphant nation, on the

14

other a groaning people, and notwithstanding the noble lord, secure on the pedestal of power, may wield in one hand the keys of St. Peter, and . . . [*Here the Hon Member was interrupted with such loud and incessant bursts of laughter that it was impossible to know whether he really closed his sentence or not. The Hon Member concluded in these words:*] Now, Mr Speaker, we see the philosophical prejudices of man. [*Laughter and cheers*] 'I respect cheers, even when they come from the lips of political opponents. [*Renewed laughter*] I think, sir . . . [*'Hear, hear,' and repeated cries of 'Question! Question!'*] I am not at all surprised, sir, at the reception which I have received. [*Continued laughter*] I have begun several times many things [*laughter*] and I have often succeeded at last. [*Fresh cries of, 'Question!'*] Ay, sir, and though I sit down now, the time will come when you will hear me! [*The Hon Member delivered the last sentence in a very loud tone, and resumed his seat.*]

Morning Chronicle, 8 December 1837

K Disraeli's outspoken comments on political issues aroused the bitter animosity of Daniel O'Connell, the leader of the Irish MPs in the Commons.

[Disraeli] is a living lie; and the British empire is degraded by tolerating a miscreant of his abominable description. . . I can find no harsher epithets in the English language by which to convey the utter abhorrence which I entertain for such a reptile. . . He possesses all the necessary requisites of perfidy, selfishness, depravity, want of principle, &c. . . His name shows that he is of Jewish origin. I do not use it as a term of reproach; there are many most respectable Jews. But there are, as in every other people, some of the lowest and most disgusting grade of moral turpitude; and of those I look upon Mr Disraeli as the worst. He has just the qualities of the impenitent thief on the Cross, and I verily believe, if Mr Disraeli's family herald were to be examined, and his genealogy traced, the same personage would be discovered to be the heir at law of the exalted individual to whom I allude. I forgive Mr Disraeli now, and as the lineal descendant of the blasphemous robber who ended his career beside the Founder of the Christian Faith, I leave the gentleman to the enjoyment of his infamous distinction and family honours.

from a report of O'Connell's speech in the *Courier*, 6 May 1835

L Disraeli replied in kind

[O'Connell] is the hired instrument of the Papacy; as such his mission is to destroy your Protestant society . . . humbling himself in the mud before a simple priest.

There was no hypocrisy in this, no craft. The agent recognised his principal, the slave bowed before his Lord; and when he pressed to his lips those robes, reeking with whisky and redolent of incense, I doubt not that his soul was filled at the same time with unaffected awe and devout gratitude.

from a letter of Disraeli's, 2 February 1836

M Disraeli explains the strategy behind Young England
The Government of Sir Robert Peel is at this moment upheld by an apparent majority in the Commons of 90 members. It is known that among these 90 are between 40 and 50 agricultural malcontents who, though not prepared to commence an active opposition, will often be absent on questions which, though not of vital, may yet be of great importance to the Minister. It is obvious therefore that another section of Conservative members, full of youth and energy and constant in their seats, must exercise an irresistible control over the tone of the Minister.

from Disraeli's 'Very Confidential' Memorandum to the King of the French, 1842

N Disraeli attacks Peel's Government over the weakness of its Irish policy
There are some measures which to introduce is disgraceful and which to oppose is degrading. I have given no vote on this [Irish Arms] Bill one way or the other and I shall continue that course, being perfectly persuaded of its futility. Believing that Ireland is governed in a manner which conduces only to the injury of both countries; believing that the old principles of the party with which I am connected are quite competent, if pursued, to do that, I hope the time will come when a party framed on true principles will do justice to Ireland, not by satisfying agitators, not by adopting in despair the first quack remedy that is offered from either side of the House, but by really penetrating into the mystery of this great misgovernment, so as to bring about a state of society which will be advantageous both to England and Ireland and which will put an end to a state of things that is the bane of England and the opprobrium of Europe.

from Disraeli's speech in the House of Commons, August 1843

O Peel's Home Secretary, condemns the personal motivation behind Disraeli's attacks upon his leader
With respect to Young England, the puppets are moved by Disraeli, who is the ablest man among them: I consider him unprincipled and disappointed and in despair he has tried the affect of bullying. I think

with you that they [the Young England members] will return to the crib after prancing, capering, and snorting; but a crack or two of the whip well applied may hasten and insure their return. Disraeli alone is mischievous; and with him I have no desire to keep terms. It would be better for the party if he were driven into the ranks of our open enemies.

from Sir James Graham to J Croker, 1843

P In 1843 Disraeli appealed to Sir James Graham to use his influence to obtain a post for one of his relations. Graham refused and informed Peel. Peel expressed his low opinion of Disraeli
I am very glad that Mr Disraeli has asked for an office for his brother. It is a good thing when such a man puts his shabbiness on record. He asked me for office himself, and I was not surprised that being refused he became independent and a patriot. But to ask favours after his conduct last session is too bad. However, it is a bridle in his mouth!

from Peel to Graham, December 1843

Q Disraeli accuses Peel of betraying his Party
If we think the opinions of the Anti-Corn Law League are dangerous . . . it is open in a free country like England for men who hold opposite views to resist them with the same earnestness, by all legitimate means. . . But what happens in this country? A body of gentlemen, able and adroit men, come forward, and profess contrary doctrines to those of these new economists. They place themselves at the head of that great popular party who are adverse to the new ideas, and, professing their opinions, they climb and clamber into power by having accepted, or rather by having eagerly sought the trust. . .

We trusted to others – to one who, by accepting or, rather, by seizing that post, obtained the greatest place in the country, and at this moment governs England. . . I think the right Hon Baronet may congratulate himself on his complete success in having entirely deceived his party.

from a speech by Disraeli in the House of Commons, 15 May 1846

R Disraeli's impact on the political scene
His appointment to this post was one of the most startling domestic events which has occurred in our time. People seemed never tired of talking and speculating on it, with its recondite causes and its problematical results. He at once became an inexhaustible topic of animated discussion in society. His portrait was painted by one

fashionable artist; his bust was taken in marble by another; what were called likenesses of him appeared in illustrated newspapers by the dozen; and above all, he was placed in Madame Tussaud's repository – that British Valhalla in which it is difficult for a civilian to gain a niche without being hanged. He glittered in the political horizon as a star of the first magnitude.

from the *Edinburgh Review*, 1853

S A contemporary political commentator describes Gladstone's eminence
[The budget] had raised Gladstone to a great political elevation and, what is of far greater significance than the measure itself, has given the country the assurance of a *man* equal to great political necessities and fit to lead parties and direct governments.

from the *Memoirs* of Charles Greville for December 1853

T Gladstone's first reaction on being made Prime Minister in 1868
I was standing by him holding his coat on my arm while he in his shirt sleeves was wielding an axe to cut down a tree. Up came a telegraph messenger. He took the telegram, opened it and read it, then handed it to me, speaking only two words, 'Very significant', and at once resumed his work. The message merely stated that General Grey would arrive that evening from Windsor. This of course implied that a mandate was coming from the Queen charging Mr Gladstone with the formation of his first government. . .

After a few minutes the blows ceased, and Mr Gladstone, resting on the handle of his axe, looked up and with deep earnestness in his voice and with great intensity in his face, explained, 'My mission is to pacify Ireland.' He then resumed his task, and never said another word till the tree was down.

from an article by Evelyn Ashley in the *National Review*, June 1869

Questions

1 What characteristics of Gladstone's earlier political attitudes are illustrated in Sources A – D? **(7 marks)**

2 How far are the differences in personality between Disraeli and Gladstone indicated by Sources E, F and H? **(7 marks)**

3 In what ways do Sources I – L reveal the problems which confronted Disraeli in establishing himself as a politician? **(7 marks)**

4 Compare Sources M and Q as evidence of the early rivalry between Gladstone and Disraeli. **(9 marks)**

5 Using your own knowledge and the evidence in Sources R – T, suggest reasons why the office of Chancellor of the Exchequer played such an important role in the political rise of Gladstone and Disraeli. **(10 marks)**

2 DISRAELI AND THE SECOND REFORM BILL, 1867

In the 1860s considerable pressure built up in Parliament and outside for a further measure of Parliamentary Reform. Disraeli was not a willing reformer, but he was a political realist. He appreciated that after the Great Reform Act of 1832 further modifications of Parliament and the electoral system were unavoidable. His strategy was for the Conservative Party to take the lead in introducing the next stage. This would have the effect both of preventing reform from being too sweeping and of denying Gladstone and the Liberals the opportunity to seize the initiative [A-C].

When Gladstone introduced a Reform Bill in 1866 Disraeli led a successful attack upon it. A group of Liberal rebels (known as the 'Adullamites') voted with the Conservatives to defeat Gladstone's Bill. This brought Lord Derby into office at the head of a Conservative Government. Disraeli became Chancellor of the Exchequer [D-H].

Disraeli introduced his own Bill in 1867. Its main terms extended the vote to rate-paying householders in the boroughs. Despite his appeal to principle, Disraeli was essentially opportunist in approach. This was shown by his readiness to accept a radical amendment proposed by Grosvenor Hodgkinson which extended the franchise to some half-million 'compounders', the class of house occupiers who did not pay full rates but shared costs with their landlords. This ran counter to the basic idea of the Bill, that the right to vote should be granted only to those who were direct rate payers [G-K].

Contemporaries attributed the passing of the 1867 Reform Bill to the power of Disraeli's personality, his great skill as a Parliamentarian, and his dominance of the Conservative Government [L-O]. Modern historians tend to regard the 1867 Reform Bill as essentially a measure designed to safeguard the electoral interests of the Conservative Party rather than as a genuine broadening of the representative character of Parliament. Similarly, in contradiction to Disraeli's high-sounding claim, they interpret his role as one of political expediency rather than idealism, and suggest that personal ambition was his chief motivation [P-S].

A Disraeli accepts the idea of limited reform

All that has occurred, all that I have observed, all the results of my reflections, lead me to this more and more: that the principle upon which the constituencies of this country should be increased is one, not of radical, but I would say, of lateral reform – the extension of the franchise, not its degradation.

I think it is possible to increase the electoral body of the country, if the opportunity were favourable and the necessity urgent, by the introduction of votes upon principles in unison with the principles of the Constitution, so that the suffrage should remain a privilege, and not a right; a privilege to be gained by virtue, by intelligence, by industry, by integrity, and to be exercised for the common good. And I think if you quit that ground, if you once admit that a man has a right to vote whom you cannot prove to be disqualified for it, you would change the character of the Constitution, and you would change it in a manner which will tend to lower the importance of this country.

from a speech in the House of Commons in 1865
on the Baines (Reform) Bill

B Disraeli introduces his Reform Bill in 1867

C Disraeli is congratulated on his opposition to democracy
You will not, I hope, be offended that I presume to thank you for your speech on the Baines (Reform) Bill. The sentiments and the language were worthy of each other, and a masterly protest against any truckling to democracy. I believe that, in proportion as a man is a

deep, sincere and consistent lover of social, civil, and religious liberty, he will be a deep, sincere and consistent hater of pure democracy, as adverse to all three.

You well showed that America, France, Australia, may endure convulsions, and partially recover from them; but England rests entirely on her institutions.

We have, however, made a great advance towards safety and satisfaction, when so many of all classes and opinions seem to agree that the franchise may be largely extended without being degraded.

Lord Shaftesbury to Disraeli, 10 May 1865

D Disraeli's tactics

[Disraeli] made a capital speech, reciting the history of the Reform Bills since 1852; throwing all the blame of the present agitation upon WEG [Gladstone]; objecting principally to the county franchise proposed in this Bill – especially the admission of copyholders and leaseholders in boroughs to vote for the counties – and still more to the fragmentary character of the measure. He said it was obviously our duty unanimously to oppose the Bill on the second reading, but that we must leave it to our leaders to decide in what form the opposition had better be made, having reference especially to the feelings and dispositions of our friends on the other side.

Lord Northcote, March 1866

E Disraeli gives his reasons for opposing the Bill

I do not believe the question of Parliamentary Reform is thoroughly understood by the country, is thoroughly understood by the House, and, although I dare only utter it in a whisper, I do not believe that it is thoroughly understood by Her Majesty's Government. I often remember with pleasure a passage in Plato, where the great sage descants upon what he calls 'double ignorance' – that is, when a man is ignorant that he is ignorant. But, Sir, there is another kind of ignorance that is fatal. There is in the first place an ignorance of principles and in the second place an ignorance of facts. And that is our position in dealing with this important question. There is not a majority in this House that can decide upon the principles upon which we ought to legislate in regard to this matter; there is not a man in this House who has at command any reliable facts upon which he can decide those principles. The country, the House of Commons, the Ministry, are . . . 'in a scrape'. We must help the Government. We must forget the last two months. The right honourable gentleman must recross the Rubicon; we must rebuild his bridges and supply him with vessels.

from a speech by Disraeli made to the Commons, May 1866

F Disraeli rejects the notion of universal suffrage in favour of the aristocratic principle
The moment you have universal suffrage, it always happens that the man who elects despises the elected. He says, 'I am as good as he is, and although I sent him to Parliament, I have not a better opinion than I have of myself'. . . There will be no charm of tradition; no families of historic lineage. . . Instead of these, you will have a horde of selfish and obscure mediocrities. . .

I think this House of Commons should remain a House of Commons, and not become a House of the People, the House of a mere indeterminate multitude, devoid of any definite character, and not responsible to society.

from a speech by Disraeli made in the Commons, May 1866

G Derby tells Disraeli that the Conservatives must undertake reform
I am coming reluctantly to the conclusion that we shall have to deal with the question of Reform. I wish you would consider whether, after all the failures which have taken place, we might not deal with the question in the shape of resolutions, to form the basis of a future Bill. We need not make the adoption of any of the resolutions a vital question; while, if we should be beaten on some great leading principle, we should have a definite issue on which to go to the country. This is worth turning in your mind; and I should be glad to hear what you think of it.

Derby to Disraeli, September 1866

H The Queen is anxious for a settlement of the reform issue
A day or two ago General Grey brought me a note in Her Majesty's handwriting, to the effect that she was most anxious for a settlement of the question; that she would gladly render any assistance in her power; that she did not like to speak to me about it, but that her idea was to offer Lord Derby her assistance in communicating with Lord Russell and Gladstone. I thought that a formal offer might be embarrassing, as, if the Cabinet ultimately decided that it was inexpedient that any communication should be made to the Liberal Party leaders, it might be awkward to have to decline Her Majesty's gracious proposal. I thought there would be very little practical use in communicating with Lord Russell or Gladstone; that they would

only give vague promises of candid consideration, which would lead
to nothing.

Last night the Queen renewed the subject with me, saying that she
quite understood my position and could not ask me for an opinion.
She was very anxious that something should be done.

Sir Stafford Northcote (President of the Board of Trade) to Disraeli,
October 1866

I Disraeli's main aim is to outmanoeuvre the Liberals

We are entirely unpledged upon the subject [of Parliamentary
Reform]. But if no notice is taken of it in the Queen's Speech, or no
subsequent announcement of measures is made by the Leader of the
House of Commons, it is probable that an amendment of a general
character may be carried, which will replace the question in the hands
of the late Government, and they return to power not more
embarrassed by the Radicals than before.

It would seem therefore we must act. How?

It seems probable that no measure of Parliamentary Reform could
be passed by a Conservative Government except in a Parliament
where they have essentially a majority.

It may be assumed that the House of Commons is really opposed
to any violent Reform, and to any Reform of any kind which is
immediate; and the longer the decision of its opinion can be delayed,
the more likely it will be in favour of moderation and postponement.

Disraeli to Lord Derby, November 1866

J Disraeli justifies his Bill on grounds of principle

Our Bill is not framed, as was the one of last session, to enfranchise
a specific number of persons. We do not attempt that. We lay down a
principle and let that principle work; but if you ask us what will be the
result of its working, we say – although we do not wish to found our
policy upon it – that we do not apprehend the number that will be
admitted to the enjoyment of the franchise will exceed the number
contemplated by the Bill of last session . . . the proposition that we
make is founded upon a principle that is not liable to alteration.

I hear much of the struggle of parties in this House, and I hear much
of combinations that may occur, and courses that may be taken,
which may affect the fate of this Bill. All I can say on the part of my
colleagues and myself is that we have no other wish at the present
moment than, with the co-operation of this House, to bring the
question of parliamentary Reform to a settlement. . .

Generally speaking, I would say that, looking to what has occurred
since the Reform Act of 1832 was passed – to the increase of

population, the progress of industry, the spread of knowledge, and our ingenuity in the arts – we are of opinion that numbers, thoughts and feelings have since that time been created which it is desirable should be admitted within the circle of the Constitution.

from a speech made to the House of Commons, March 1867

K Disraeli explains privately why he accepted Hodgkinson's amendment extending the vote to occupiers

I waited until the question was put, when, having resolved everything in my mind, I felt that the critical moment had arrived, and when, without in the slightest degree receding from our principle and position of a rating and confidential franchise, we might take a step which would destroy the present agitation and extinguish Gladstone & Co I therefore accepted the spirit of H[odgkinson]'s amendment.

Disraeli to Gathorne Hardy, 1867

L Disraeli's control over his government colleagues

But for this power to hold his tongue, Mr Disraeli would never have got this Bill through the House. Moreover, he seems to be able to silence his colleagues' tongues, either by positive and inexorable command or by the mesmeric power of example. In reviewing the course of this Bill, it is astonishing to find how little speaking came from the Treasury Bench. . . The Chancellor of the Exchequer has ruled his Ministry with despotic power. You must speak, he seemed to say to one, and he spoke. To others he issued no commands and they were silent. . . Further, it has been remarked that, whatever may have been done in the Cabinet, in the House the leader appeared to consult none of his colleagues. . . In short, Disraeli has steered this Bill through himself; alone he did it; and with what wonderful skill none but those who watched him from night to night can know.

from a letter by a Conservative MP, W White, 1867

M Disraeli's political skill

It was in [the] course of preparing this Reform Bill of 1867 and watching every night its passage through Parliament, that I had ample means, for the first and last time, of judging of Mr D[israeli]'s characteristics. I was constantly struck by his great skill in overcoming difficulties as they arose in Parliament, and his tact in meeting, by judicious compromises, the objections of his opponents.

from a letter by T Thring, 1868

N There were those who considered that Disraeli had got the Bill through only at the expense of reversing his original position on reform

The Right Hon gentleman opposite [Disraeli] has adopted a course which is infinitely creditable to his dexterity as a tactician. He well knew that, had he proposed the measure as it is now before us and shown it to his Party at first, they would have started back from it in horror. The Right Hon gentleman has treated them as we treat a shy horse . . . take him gently up, walk him round the object . . . and then, when the process has been repeated often enough, we hope we shall get the creature to pass it quietly. . . We saw, – *he did not say this in so many words, but his speech amounted to this* – We saw from the first that the principle of personal rating and the compound-householder were things absolutely antagonistic. . . But we did not say so. No; we had a precious cargo on board, and we did not wish to overload our ship with something which might sink it.

from a speech by Robert Lowe in the Commons, May 1867

O In a celebrated public speech after the Reform Bill had been passed, Disraeli sought to clarify the motives and aims which had underlain his policy

I had to prepare the mind of the country, and to educate – if it be not arrogant to use such a phrase – to educate our Party. It is a large Party, and requires its attention to be called to questions of this kind with some pressure. I had to prepare the mind of Parliament and the country on this question of Reform. This was not only with the concurrence of Lord Derby, but of my colleagues.

When you try to settle any great question, there are two considerations which statesmen ought not to forget. First of all, let your plan be founded upon some principle. But that is not enough. Let it also be a principle that is in harmony with the manners and customs you are attempting to legislate for. . . In a progressive country change is constant; and the great question is not whether you should resist change which is inevitable, but whether that change should be carried out in deference to the manners, the customs, the laws, the traditions of the people, or in deference to abstract principles and arbitrary and general doctrines. The one is a national system; the other, to give it an epithet, a noble epithet which perhaps it may deserve, is a philosophic system. Both have great advantages; the national party is supported by the fervour of patriotism; the philosophical party has a singular exemption from the force of prejudice.

from a speech by Disraeli made in Edinburgh in 1867

P Disraeli – a skilled improviser

It is often believed that Disraeli, infinitely more discerning than the dull squires who followed him, had long perceived that household suffrage would enfranchise a class basically more Conservative than the electorate created in 1832; that he aimed throughout at this objective, carrying Derby with him and educating the rest of the Party in the process. . .

It is probably true that the Reform Bill did in the end enfranchise a class which for a number or reasons tended to vote Conservative rather than Liberal. It is also true that Disraeli, more than any other statesman of his day, had the imagination to adapt himself to this new situation and to discern, dimly and hesitatingly perhaps, what the artisan class wanted from Parliament. . . But there is nothing – or very little – to suggest that he had any such awareness in 1867. The importance of that period in his life is quite different. In the course of two years from the summer of 1865 he transformed his position in the Conservative Party. It was his sparkling success in the session of 1867 which made him, as he had by no means been before, Derby's inevitable successor. . .

For what he did in 1867 he deserves to go down in history as a politician of genius, a superb improviser, a parliamentarian of unrivalled skill, but not as a far-sighted statesman or the educator of his party.

from *Disraeli* by Robert Blake (1966)

Q Disraeli's real motives

The motives that now governed the Conservative leaders, and the tactics that were pursued by Disraeli especially, in the twelve months down to the passing of the final Act, have been analysed in almost microscopic detail by a group of recent historians [F B Smith, *The Making of the Second Reform Bill*, (1966); Maurice Cowling, *1867 Disraeli, Gladstone and Revolution*, (1967); Royden Harrison, *Before the Socialists: Studies in Labour and Politics 1861–1881*, (1965)]. As a result, a whole mythology has been virtually destroyed. It is now clear that Disraeli's attitude during the Reform crisis was purely opportunist. He neither sought to 'educate his party', nor displayed either firmness or consistency of purpose in his support for 'democracy'. Indeed, during these months Disraeli had only one major aim: to destroy Gladstone's leadership over a united Liberal Party, and, by seizing the initiative in reform himself and promoting a Reform Bill, to consolidate his own leadership of the Conservative Party. . .

To many contemporaries, both of Left and Right, the Second Reform Act seemed to be an essentially democratic measure which gave effective political power to the working class. Superficially this appeared to be true. Nearly a million new voters were added to the electoral list, and the increase was widest in the great cities where working-class voters now became a majority. But the position in the counties was very different, and does much to justify Mr Cowling's remark that Disraeli 'was prepared to let Radicals have their way in the boroughs, so long as he had his to some extent in the counties'.

from *Gladstone, Disraeli and Later Victorian Politics* by P Adelman (1970)

R Disraeli had preserved Conservative Party interests
The circumstances which the Conservatives most feared gained little [from the redistribution measures that accompanied the 1867 Act]. London, which on a weighting for its electorate might have expected some 60 extra members, received only a handful. . . The measures of 1867–68 were notable . . . for how little they changed the old pattern of constituencies and the social balance of county politics. The established interests among which the Conservatives were so strongly represented had escaped relatively unscathed.

from *Conservatism and the Conservative Party in Nineteenth-Century Britain* by B Coleman (1988)

S Disraeli had defended the landed interest
The Second Reform Act provides a further illustration of Disraeli's concern to use a necessary measure of reform to sustain the threatened power and flagging fortunes of the landed interest. It was expressly intended to make the electoral world a more congenial place for Conservatives. The extension of the franchise to male householders (and some lodgers) in the boroughs, which brought an enormous increase in the number of working-class voters, was the main focus of heated controversy at the time, but the important thing for Disraeli and his party was to sustain and strengthen the influence of the landed Conservatism of the counties and the small boroughs.

from *Disraeli* by John K Walton (1990)

Questions

1 To what extent do Sources A, C, D, E and F suggest that Disraeli's attitude towards reform had more to do with tactics than principle?
(7 marks)

2 In what ways do Sources G–H indicate the pressures on Disraeli in regard to the reform issue? **(8 marks)**

3 How far do Sources I – K reveal a contradictory approach to reform on Disraeli's part? **(7 marks)**

4 Does the evidence in Sources L – O support or challenge Disraeli's assertion in Source O (line 2) that his aim in introducing the 1867 Reform Bill had been 'to educate our party'? **(8 marks)**

5 How closely do the historians quoted in Sources P – S agree in their assessment of Disraeli's motives in introducing reform? **(10 marks)**

3 GLADSTONE'S FIRST MINISTRY, 1868–74

The years 1868–74 marked one of the great reforming periods in modern British history. Often referred to as 'The high tide of Liberalism', Gladstone's first ministry undertook a wide range of legislative reforms which affected nearly all the major institutions in the state. The army, the universities, the legal system, the trade unions, the voting system, the civil service, the licensing system, education: all these underwent significant modification. In addition, Ireland pressed heavily upon the Government and was the subject of a set of major reforms.

The reform of the British Army was a response to the military victories of the Prussian Army in Europe in the 1860s and 1870s, which both impressed and disturbed Britain. An important feature of the reforms, introduced by Edward Cardwell, Gladstone's War Secretary, was the implementation of the principle of promotion based on merit, and the abolition of the practice whereby commissions were sold to the highest bidder [A-B].

In the second half of the nineteenth century there was general agreement on the need for the extension of a national system of elementary education, but deep disagreement as to the method of achieving it. At base, the problem was a religious one. Until the 1870s schooling had largely been supplied by the established Anglican Church which argued through its representative body, The National Education Union, that educational reforms should strengthen the position and funding of the existing denominational 'voluntary' schools. This body was strongly opposed by the National Education League, a nonconformist organisation, which objected vehemently to the idea of state funds being used to support the teaching of Anglican doctrines. The Education Bill, introduced in 1870 by W.E. Forster, was intended as a compromise between the demands of the Anglican 'voluntaryists' and the nonconformists. The Bill satisfied neither side. The nonconformists, previously one of the strongest groups among Liberal supporters, revolted against it [C-G].

The Liberal measures relating to the reform of Trade Union Law also brought a mixed response. While the Trade Union Act of 1871 granted the unions new legal rights and protection, the Criminal Law Amendment Act of the same year outlawed picketing, the only means of making strikes effective. What had been offered to the unions with one hand seemed to have been taken away with the other [H-I].

The unprecedented range of the reforms introduced during Gladstone's first ministry was both an achievement and a liability. Each of them offended a particular vested interest, with the result that as the ministry continued it met increasing opposition [J-L]. A measure which aroused especially fierce resistance was the 1872 reform of the Licensing Laws. The restriction on the opening hours of, and the rights of admission to, public houses was intended to combat the seriously anti-social consequences of uncontrolled alcoholic drinking. Opponents of the Act, however, condemned the legislation as a encroachment on individual liberty and commerical freedom [M-N].

Modern scholars, while acknowledging the significance of the 1868–74 Liberal Ministry, tend to see the reforms as products of pragmatism rather then systematic planning. They emphasise the insoluble problems that weakened all Liberal Governments in the nineteenth century [O-P].

A Gladstone justifies the abolition of the sale of army commissions

I should like to assure myself that you really have the points of the case before you. *1.* Was it not for us an indispensable duty to extinguish a gross, wide-spread, and most mischievous illegality, of which the existence had become certain and notorious? *2.* Was it not also our duty to extinguish it in the best manner? *3.* Was not the best manner that which, (*a*) made the extinction final; (*b*) gave the best, ie a statutory, title for regulation prices; (*c*) granted an indemnity to the officers; (*d*) secured for them compensation in respect of over-regulation prices? *4.* Did not the vote of the House of Lords stop us in this best manner of proceeding? *5.* Did it absolve us from the duty of putting an end to the illegality? *6.* What method of putting an end to it remained to us, except that which we have adopted?

Gladstone to Lord Lyttleton, July 1871

B A Liberal supporter explains Gladstone's motives

[In] abolishing purchase by a royal warrant Mr Gladstone acted strictly within the terms of an act of parliament, an act so modern as the reign of George III. He in truth followed a course which that act not only allowed but rather suggested. . . I believe that it was better to get rid of a foul abuse in the way in which it was got rid of, than not to get rid of it at all, especially as the House of Commons had already decided against it. Still, the thing did not look well. It might seem that by electing to bring a bill into parliament Mr Gladstone had waived his right to employ the royal power in the matter. . . I believe that this is one of those cases in which a strictly conscientious man like Mr Gladstone does things from which a less conscientious man would shrink. Such a man, fully convinced of his own integrity, often thinks less than it would be wise to think of mere appearances, and so lays himself open to the imputation of motives poles asunder from the real ones.

E A Freeman in the *Pall Mall Gazette*, 12 February 1874

C The Anglican view on education
There was at present great voluntary support to schools; it was a matter of charity; and the burden was very unequal, because it varied according to the charitable feeling of individuals. Even these persons, at times, were conscious of the burden and of its inequality; so that under this Bill many would resort to rates to save their subscriptions ... such a system would put an end not only to voluntary subscriptions but also, as a consequence, to that interest in education which ought to be felt throughout the whole community. . .

The late Report on the state of education in four of our great towns had showed that the Church had done nearly everything there. It had established good schools, and carried them on quietly and unostentatiously for years. If anyone desired to know which religious body was the most earnest in the cause of education, let him consult any one of the Reports of the Committee of Council, and he would see how churchmen had laboured, what large sums they had expended, and how many schools they maintained. . .

from speeches of Robert Montagu, the Conservative spokesman on education, in the House of Commons, February and March 1870

D The Nonconformist view
The present system of aid from Parliamentary grants was intended to be an experiment. . . The National Education League proposes to supplement this system by one which shall be national, universal, and certain – which shall be independent of the accidents of wealth and benevolence – which shall impose upon all an obligation which should be felt by all. . . We hope to attain these results by making education national, compulsory, unsectarian and free. . . we hope to found a national system. . . What do we mean by a national system? We mean one which shall be supported by the nation, and shall belong to the nation. But it is said we are a country of different sects and different beliefs – you cannot found any 'national' system which does not take account of these. That is a very good argument against the existence of a National Church; but it is no argument against a system of national education, which has nothing to do with creeds and tenets. . .

from a lecture by Francis Adams, Secretary of the National Education League, February 1870

E Forster proposes an Education Bill

We have said that we must have provision for public elementary schools. The first question then is, by whom is it to be made? . . . To see, then, whether voluntary help will be forth-coming we give a year. . . If that zeal, if that willingness, does not come forward to supply the schools that are required, then the children must no longer remain untaught, and the State must step in. . . I have said that there will be compulsory provision where it is wanted . . . but not otherwise. . . How do we propose to apply it? By School Boards elected by the district. We have already got the district; we have found out the educational want existing in it – we see that the district must be supplied – we have waited in the hope that some persons would supply it; they have not done so. We, therefore, say that it must be supplied; but by whom? . . . Voluntary local agency has failed, therefore, our hope is to invoke the help of municipal organisation. Therefore, where we have proved the educational need we supply it by local administration – that is, by means of rates aided by money voted by Parliament.

from W E Forster's House of Commons speech, March 1870

" OBSTRUCTIVES."

Mr. Punch (to Bull A B). " YES, IT'S ALL VERY WELL TO SAY, 'GO TO SCHOOL!' HOW ARE THEY TO GO TO SCHOOL WITH THOSE PEOPLE QUARRELLING IN THE DOORWAY? WHY DON'T YOU MAKE 'EM 'MOVE ON'?"

F 'Obstructives': a Punch cartoon, 2 July 1870

G The Nonconformist Revolt

The Government has chosen deliberately to defy us. . . This conduct leaves us no alternative. . . The great principle of religious equality must be accepted as part of the Programme of any Party which in future seeks our support and alliance. The 'Nonconformist Revolt' long threatened has begun.

from a speech by Joseph Chamberlain in 1870

H The benefits to the unions of the 1871 Trade Union Act

This Act is now well known, and therefore it is only needful to merely indicate the changes effected by it. For the first time in history the Act of 1871 made combinations – trade unions – lawful giving to them advantages which had hitherto been denied to them. The law, as it stood, was so intricate and slippery that a bare enactment legalizing trade unions was deemed to be impossible. They had to be legalized by special enactment, making them lawful associations, with a certain legal status in courts of law, and at the same time preserve their internal economy, of organisation and management, from mischievous interference by litigation.

from Labour Legislation (1902) by George Howell

I The disadvantages to the unions of the 1871 Criminal Law Amendment

The judges . . . declared that the only effect of the legislation of 1871 was to make the trade objects of the strike not illegal. A strike was perfectly legal; but if the means employed were calculated to coerce the employer they were illegal means, and a combination to do a legal act by illegal means was a criminal conspiracy. In other words a strike was lawful but anything done in pursuance of a strike was criminal. Thus the judges tore up a remedial statute (the Trade Union Act), and each fresh decision went further and developed new dangers.

from Digest of Labour Laws by H Crompton and F Harrison (1872)

J The underlying aim of the Liberal Government's Civil Service reforms was to attract talent to the Service by means of open competition

Except as hereinafter is excepted, all appointments which it may be necessary to make, after the 31st day of August next, to any of the situations included, or to be included, in Schedule A to this Order annexed, shall be made by means of competitive examinations, according to regulations to be from time to time framed by the said Civil Service Commissioners, and approved by the Commissioners of Her Majesty's Treasury, open to all persons (of the requisite age, health, character, and other qualifications prescribed in the said regulations) who may be desirous of attending the same, subject to the payment of such fees as the said Civil Service Commissioners, with the consent of the said Commissioners of Her Majesty's Treasury, may from time to time require.

from the Orders in Council, June 1870

K Gladstone had for some time been in favour of the ballot (secret voting) in Parliamentary elections

I have at all times given my vote in favour of open voting, but I have done so before, and I do so now, with an important reservation, namely, that whether by open voting or by whatever means, free voting must be secured.

from a speech of Gladstone's, December 1868

L The Ballot Act, 1872

In the case of a poll at an election the votes shall be given by ballot. The ballot of each voter shall consist of a paper (in this Act called a ballot paper) showing the names and description of the candidates.

The voter will go into one of the compartments, and, with the pencil provided in the compartment, place a cross on the right-hand side opposite the name of each candidate for whom he votes, thus X.

The voter will then fold up the ballot paper so as to show the official mark on the back, and leaving the compartment will, without showing the front of the paper to any person, show the official mark on the back to the presiding officer, and then, in the presence of the presiding officer, put the paper into the ballot box, and forthwith quit the polling station.

from an Act to amend the law relating to procedure at Parliamentary and Municipal Elections, July 1872

M The reaction of the trade to the Licensing Act

The Licensing Act of 1872 has proved injurious alike to the people and the Trade. It tends to demoralise the former and it destroys the property of the latter. . .

The comfort of the people and the liberty of the subject it totally disregards.

from the *Licensed Victuallers' Guardian*, November 1872

N The power of beer and gin

No Ministry, however strong, and however pressed from the outside by fanatical agitators, would willingly provoke an opposition so formidable as that with which the publican interest threatens every Administration that dares to meddle with the traffic in strong drinks. It is painful and discreditable to be compelled to confess that in so many recent elections the power of 'Beer' has turned the scale, and it is only too probable that whenever Parliament may be dissolved the brewing and distilling interest will command as many votes as ever the old Whig connexion in the palmiest days of close boroughs had under its control. . . It turns elections and shakes Administrations, and is courted by parties. . . For it must be remembered that Beer was once a great Liberal power, as surely to be reckoned on the Liberal side as Land was to be reckoned on the Conservative side. It is only in our day that the Tories find their safest if not their ablest candidates among the scions of the great brewing and distilling firms.

from *The Economist*, December 1873

O The growing difficulties facing Gladstone's Government provided Disraeli with the opportunity to ridicule his rivals

As time advanced it was not difficult to perceive that extravagance was being substituted for energy by the Government. The unnatural stimulus was subsiding. Their paroxysms ended in prostration. Some took refuge in melancholy, and their eminent chief alternated between a menace and a sigh. As I sat opposite the Treasury Bench the Ministers reminded me of one of those marine landscapes not very uncommon on the coasts of South America. You behold a range of exhausted volcanoes. Not a flame flickers on a single pallid crest. But the situation is still dangerous. There are occasional earthquakes, and ever and anon the dark rumbling of the sea.

from a speech by Disraeli, April 1872

P A modern view of Gladstone's problems

Gladstone had spent much of his [1868–74] administration in conflict with his colleagues and with groups in his party both 'left' and 'right', but when it came to the point, they could not let him go. The Liberal party aspired to classlessness, but it was riddled with class; it hoped for interdenominationalism, but it divided between . . . sectarianism and secularism; it tried to offer justice to the three kingdoms but it satisfied none. Gladstone stood outside the Cabinet and the party; his class was indefinable, his religion exceptional; he was an extreme Radical on some questions, an unreconstructed Conservative on others; he was at the same time a chief architect of the mid-nineteenth-century settlement and seen as one of the chief threats to its continuation. Disraeli was self-evidently exotic, but viewed from the perspective of any one of the groups that constituted the Liberal party, so was Gladstone.

In the decades after the start of household suffrage, British political parties slowly, surprisingly slowly, and in the case of the Liberals only in part, took on those attributes characteristic of a modern party: bureaucracy and caution. But during the transitional phase, exceptional demands were made of their leaders and especially of the leader of the Liberal party as it struggled to preserve its identity caught between the certainty of a property-based Conservative party and the uncertainty of developments 'to the left'. . .

Gladstone's first government petered out, never recovering from the abortive resignation of March 1873. In this it followed the Liberal stereo-type: every Liberal government between 1830 and 1895 ended by the disintegration of its own support in the Commons.

from *Gladstone 1809–74* by H C G Matthew (1988)

Q Gladstone had been aware of these problems
The condition of the liberal party requires consideration:

(*a*) It has no present public *cause* upon which it is agreed.

(*b*) It has serious & conscientious divisions of opinion, which are also pressing, eg on Education.

(*c*) The habit of making a career by & upon constant active opposition to the bulk of the party, & its leaders, has acquired a dangerous predominance among a portion of its members. This habit is not checked by the action of the great majority, who do not indulge or approve it: & it has become dangerous to the credit & efficiency of the party.

from a March 1874 entry in *The Gladstone Diaries*

Questions

1 What insights do Sources A and B, and J–K, offer into the motives behind the reforms of the period 1868–74? **(7 marks)**

2 How effectively do Sources D, E and G illustrate the issues involved in the debate on educational reform in this period? **(7 marks)**

3 Using your own knowledge, and the evidence in Sources H, I, J and N, explain the reasons for the growing unpopularity of Gladstone's first ministry during its own time. **(8 marks)**

4 Does your own knowledge, and the evidence in these Sources, bear out the suggestion that the reforms introduced during Gladstone's first ministry were 'the products of pragmatism rather than systematic planning' (page 31, lines 9–10)? **(9 marks)**

5 What light do Sources P and Q throw on the problems confronting the Liberal Party under Gladstone? **(9 marks)**

4 DISRAELI AND CONSERVATISM

As a young politician Disraeli built his career on attacking Peel, the leader who had transformed the Tory Party into the Conservative Party. However, within a year of denouncing Peel's 1846 repeal of the Corn Laws, Disraeli publicly declared his acceptance of the measure [A].

Twenty years later, having risen to the top of the Conservative Party, Disraeli followed policies that were essentially Peelite. He accepted the need for measured, controlled reform and of adjusting policies in the light of social and economic change. It was not that he welcomed these changes, but that he calculated that it would be far less disruptive and threatening if the traditional ruling classes were to initiate the reforms that could not be resisted. In this way they would remain in control of the political situation. He was willing to be associated with the notion of 'Tory Democracy', but always with the intention of preventing democracy from running to extremes [C-F].

Disraeli's involvement in the passing of the 1867 Reform Act considerably advanced his position in the Conservative Party, but there remained a significant number of Conservatives who distrusted him [G].

Disraeli's great opportunity to impose himself on the Conservative Party, and for Conservatism to win over the nation, came with Gladstone's first ministry, 1868–74. In a series of campaign speeches in the early 'seventies', Disraeli portrayed the Liberal Reforms as an attack upon the traditional character of Britain. He played upon the fears of the propertied and commerical classes by suggesting that Gladstone was an irrational demagogue, hell-bent on destroying British Institutions [H-J].

With the defeat of the Liberals in 1874, Disraeli became Prime Minister again. For the next six years he headed a ministry which was no less significant than its predecessor in its legislative achievements. Social reform was high on the agenda [P-Q].

A Disraeli's belated acceptance of the repeal of the Corn Laws

The maintenance of the agricultural industry of the Country is the necessary condition of the enjoyment of the Constitution. . .

Influenced by this principle, I offered, during the recent assault on our protective system, a faithful, though fruitless, opposition to that project. . .

I am not, however, one of those who would counsel, or who would abet, any attempt factiously and forcibly to repeal the measures of

AT LAST.

4th March, 1868.

B Disraeli climbs to the top of the greasy pole

1846. The legislative sanction which they have obtained, requires that they should receive an ample experiment; and I am persuaded that this test alone can satisfy the nation either of their expediency, or their want of fitness.

from Disraeli's Buckingham election address, 25 May 1847

C Disraeli defines the role of the Tory Party

In a progressive country change is constant; and the great question is not whether you should resist change which is inevitable, but whether that change should be carried out in deference to the manners, the customs, the laws, and the traditions of a people, or whether it should be carried out in deference to abstract principles, and arbitrary and general doctrines. The one is a national system; the other, to give it an epithet, a noble epithet – which it may perhaps deserve – is a philosophic system. Both have great advantages; the national party is supported by the fervour of patriotism; the philosophic party has a singular exemption from the force of prejudice.

Now, my lords and gentlemen, I have always considered that the Tory Party was the national party of England. It is not formed of a combination of oligarchs and philosophers who practise on the sectarian prejudices of a portion of the people. It is formed of all classes from the highest to the most homely, and it upholds a series of institutions that are in theory, and ought to be in practice, an embodiment of the national requirements and the security of national rights. Whenever the Tory Party degenerates into an oligarchy it becomes unpopular; whenever the institutions do not fulfil their original intention, the Tory Party becomes odious; but when the people are led by their natural leaders, and when, by their united influence, the national institutions fulfil their original intention, the Tory Party is triumphant, and then under Providence will secure the prosperity and power of the country.

from a speech by Disraeli in Edinburgh, 1867

D Disraeli claims that the Tory Party represents the nation

The Tory Party has resumed its natural functions in the government of the country. For what is the Tory Party unless it represents national feeling? If it does not represent national feeling, Toryism is nothing. It does not depend upon hereditary coteries of nobles. It does not attempt power by attracting to itself the spurious force which may accidentally arise from advocating cosmopolitan principles or talking cosmopolitan jargon. The Tory Party is nothing unless it can represent and uphold the institutions of the country. I cannot help believing that my Lord Derby and his colleagues have taken a happy opportunity to enlarge the privileges of the people of England. We have not done anything but strengthen the institutions of the country, the essence of whose force is that they represent the interests and guard the rights of the people.

from a speech at the Mansion House, 1867

E By the early 1860s Disraeli had developed the argument that Liberalism was a matter of passing political fashion whereas Conservatism represented permanence and stability
To build up a community, not upon Liberal principles which anyone may fashion to his fancy, but upon popular principles, which assert equal rights, civil and religious; to uphold the institutions of the country because they are embodiments of the wants and wishes of the nation; equally to resist democracy and oligarchy, and favour that principle of free aristocracy which is the only basis and security for constitutional government; to be vigilant to guard and prompt to vindicate the honour of the country, but to hold aloof from that turbulent diplomacy which only distracts the mind of a people from internal improvement; to lighten taxation; frugally but wisely to administer the public treasure; to favour popular education, because it is the best guarantee for public order; to defend local government, and to be as jealous of the rights of the workingman as of the prerogative of the Crown and the privilege of the Senate – these were once the principles which regulated Tory statesmen, and I, for one, have no wish that the Tory Party should ever be in power unless they practise them.

from a speech of Disraeli's in 1862

F In 1870 Disraeli specified the purpose of the Conservative Party and the tasks confronting it
To change back the oligarchy into a generous aristocracy round a real throne; to infuse life and vigour into the Church as the trainer of the nation . . . to emancipate the political constituency of 1832 from its sectarian bondage and contracted sympathies; to elevate the physical as well as the moral condition of the people, by establishing that labour required regulation as much as property; and all this rather by the use of ancient forms and the restoration of the past than by political revolutions founded on abstract ideas, appeared to be the course which the circumstances of this country required, and which, practically speaking, could only, with all their faults and backslidings, be undertaken and accomplished by a reconstructed Tory Party.

from the General Preface to an 1870 edition of Disraeli's novels

G Conservative doubts about Disraeli

As far as I can judge the one object for which they, the Conservative Party, are striving heartily is the premiership of Mr Disraeli. If I had a firm confidence in his principles or his honesty, or even if he were identified by birth or property with the Conservative classes in the country – I might in the absence of any definite professions work to maintain him in power. But he is an adventurer: and as I have good cause to know, he is without principles and honesty.

You will say I am giving greater prominence to a question of mere personal esteem. It is true: But in this matter the personal question is the whole question. Mr Disraeli's great talent and singular power of intrigue make his practically master of the movements of his Party. It was shown as clearly as possible last year. The conversion of the Cabinet and the Party to household suffrage was a feat which showed that there was nothing strong enough in either to resist his will. For all practical purposes Mr Disraeli for the time being at least is the Conservative Party. The worst alternative that can happen is his continuance in power. He is under a temptation to Radical measures to which no other Minister is subject: because he can only remain in power by bringing stragglers from his adversary's army – and the stragglers are the men of extreme opinions. He can forward Radical changes in a way that no other Minister could do – because he alone can silence and paralyse the forces of Conservatism. And in an age of singularly reckless statesmen he is, I think, beyond question the one who is least restrained by fear or scruple.

> from the Marquess of Salisbury to Mr Gaussen of the Hertfordshire Conservative Association, April 1868

H Disraeli describes Liberalism as a national threat

[The] tone and tendency of Liberalism cannot be long concealed. It is to attack the institutions of the country under the name of Reform, and to make war on the manners and customs of the people of the country under the pretext of Progress. . .

Gentlemen, I have referred to what I look upon as the first object of the Tory Party – namely, to maintain the institutions of the country, and reviewing what has occurred, and referring to the present temper of the times upon these subjects, I think the Tory Party, or, as I will venture to call it, the National party, has everything to encourage it. I think that the nation, tested by many and severe trials, has arrived at the first duty of England to maintain its institutions, because to them we principally ascribe the power and prosperity of the country. Gentlemen, there is another and second great object of the Tory Party. If you look to the history of this country since the advent of Liberalism – forty years ago – you will find that there has been no effort so continuous, so subtle, supported by so much energy, and carried on with so much ability and acumen, as the attempts of Liberalism to effect the disintegration of the Empire of England. Gentlemen, another great object of the Tory Party, and one not inferior to the maintenance of the Empire, or the upholding of our institutions, is the elevation of the condition of the people.

from a speech at Crystal Palace, June 1872

I The appeal of Conservatism to the middle class
The real truth is that the middle-class, or its effective strength, has swung round to Conservative. Conservatism no doubt it is of a vague and negative kind; but its practical effect is an undefined preference for 'leaving well alone'. When we look at the poll in the City of London, in Westminster, in Middlesex, in Surrey, in Liverpool, Manchester, Leeds and Sheffield, in the metropolitan boroughs and in the home counties, in all the centres of industry, wealth and cultivation we see one unmistakable fact, that the rich trading-class, and the comfortable middle-class has grown distinctly Conservative. There are no special causes at work in these great constituencies. Beer has no influence with the merchants, shopkeepers and citizens of London. There are no great landlords or employers in Marylebone. The Carlton Club cannot pull the wires of Manchester and Sheffield. The 25th Section men are not very strong in Westminster, and there is no 'residuum' in Hertfordshire and Essex, in Lancashire and Yorkshire counties. These great boroughs and counties contain the very flower of the men of business. The inference is unmistakable. The effective force of the middle-class has grown for a season Conservative. The Conservative Party has become as much the middle-class party as the Liberal used to be, as much and more.
   This then, appears to us the great lesson of the elections of 1874, that the middle-classes have gone over to the enemy bag and baggage.

from an article by Frederic Harrison in the *Fortnightly Review*, 1874

J Disraeli claims that Conservatism represents the working classes
The great body of the people of this country are Conservative. When I say 'Conservative' I use the word in its purest and loftiest sense. I mean that the people of England, and especially the working classes of England, are proud of belonging to a great country, and wish to maintain its greatness – that they are proud of belonging to an Imperial country, and are resolved to maintain, if they can, their Empire – that they believe, on the whole, that the greatness and the

Empire of England are to be attributed to the ancient institutions of
the land.

Public opinion appears to be in favour of our principles – that public
opinion which, I am bound to say, thirty years ago, was not favourable
to our opinions, and which during a long period of controversy, in
the interval had been doubtful.

from Disraeli's speech at the Crystal Palace, 1872

K A modern historian describes the range of Disraeli's social reforms
The list is impressive: two important Trade Union Acts; the Public
Health Act which consolidated a multitude of earlier measures; the
Artisans Dwellings Act empowering local authorities to replace slums
by adequate houses; an Agricultural Holdings Act which met, though
only partially, some of the tenants' grievances; an Act to safeguard
the funds of Friendly Societies; a Factory Act to protect women and
children against exploitation – there had already been one in the
previous session to establish the principle of the ten-hour day; and
finally the Sale of Food and Drugs Act which remained the principal
measure on that subject until 1928. No other session was quite as
productive, although the Rivers Pollution, Merchant Shipping and
Education Acts of 1876 were important, and so, too was the Factory
Act of 1878 based on the report of a Royal Commission set up two
years earlier.

from *Disraeli* by R Blake (1966)

**L Disraeli had defined his own and his Party's attitude towards social
reform during his previous campaigns against Gladstonian
Liberalism**
Gentlemen, another great object of the Tory Party, and one not inferior
to the maintenance of the Empire, or the upholding of our institutions,
is the elevation of the condition of the people. . . It must be obvious
to all who consider the condition of the multitude with a desire to
improve and elevate it, that no important step can be gained unless
you can effect some reduction in their hours of labour and humanize
their toil. . . I ventured to say a short time ago, speaking in one of the
great cities of the country, that the health of the people was the most
important question for a statesman. . . What is the opinion of the great
Liberal Party – the party that seeks to substitute cosmopolitan for
national principles in the government of this country – on this
subject. . . ? A leading member . . . denounced them the other day as
a 'policy of sewage'.

Well, it may be a 'policy of sewage' to a Liberal Member of
Parliament. But to one of the labouring multitude of England, who

has found fever to be one of the members of his household – who has, year after year, seen stricken down the children of his loins, on whose sympathy and material support he has looked with hope and confidence, it is not a 'policy of sewage', but a question of life and death . . . is it all that wonderful that they should wish to elevate and improve their condition, and is it unreasonable that they should ask the legislature to assist them in that behest as far as it is consistent with the general welfare of the realm?

from Disraeli's speech at Crystal Palace in 1872

M Soon after taking office in 1874 Disraeli declared that his Conservative Government had the interests of the working classes high on its list of priorities

I have been alarmed recently by learning, from what I suppose is the highest Liberal authority, that a Conservative Government cannot endure, because it has been returned by Conservative working men, and a Conservative working man is an anomaly. We have been told that a working man cannot be Conservative, because he has nothing to conserve – he has neither land nor capital; as if there were not other things in the world as precious as land and capital! . . . There are things in my opinion even more precious than land and capital, and without which land and capital would be of little worth. What, for instance, is land without liberty? And what is capital without justice? The working classes of this country have inherited personal rights which the nobility of other nations do not yet possess. Their persons and their homes are sacred. They have no fear of arbitrary arrests or domiciliary visits. They know that the administration of law in this country is pure, and that it is no respecter of individuals or classes. Surely these are privileges worthy of being preserved! Can we therefore be surprised that a nation which possess such rights should wish to preserve them? And if that be the case, is it wonderful that the working classes are Conservative?

from a speech of Disraeli's in 1874

N Not all contemporaries were convinced that Disraeli's commitment to social reform was wholly genuine

Lord Beaconsfield has shown from time to time imaginative sensitiveness for the sufferings of the poor. . . There is a good deal of true insight and kindly appreciation in Lord Beaconsfield's sketches of men and organisations who to the vulgar and scared rich are objects at once of terror and contempt. But the thing never goes beyond artistic sentiment. . . Lord Beaconsfield's fatal love of rank and wealth and power has made him always more ready to use the prejudices of their possessors for his own political advancement, than to combat them in the interests of persons and classes for whose sufferings he has shown tenderness . . . which . . . does little more than furnish a basis for his denunciations of Whig indifference to these things.

from the *Fortnightly Review,* 1878

O R A Cross, Home Secretary under Disraeli, recorded that his leader's interest in the details of social reform was remarkably limited

I was, I confess, disappointed at the want of originality shown by the Prime Minister. From all his speeches, I had quite expected that his mind was full of legislative schemes, but such did not prove to be the case; on the contrary, he had to rely on the various suggestions of his colleagues, and they themselves had only just come into office.

from *A Political History* by R A Cross, 1903

P This aspect of Disraeli's policies has been emphasised by Robert Blake

Whether we look at these measures from the point of view of Disraeli's career or of the history of the Conservative Party, it is important to see them in the right perspective. They certainly represented a substantial effort to redeem electoral pledges, and taken together constitute the biggest instalment of social reform passed by any one government in the nineteenth century. But it is an exaggeration to regard them as the product of a fundamentally different political philosophy from that of the Liberals, or to see in them the fulfilment of some concept of paternalistic Tory democracy which had been adumbrated by Disraeli in opposition to Peel during the 1840s and now at last had reached fruition. The forces of property, commercial and industrial as well as landed, were by 1874 too deeply rooted in the Conservative Party to make it politically possible for the party to pursue the idea of an aristocratic anti-middle class alliance with the working masses even if it had wished to do so. As a result of the Act of 1867 it was electorally necessary to make some concessions to working-class demands, and it may be that the Conservatives after 1874 were more ready to do this than the Liberals after 1868, because those demands had become more articulate. But it would be straining the evidence to go beyond that.

There is nothing discreditable in the way in which the Conservative Party arrived at these measures. Governments usually act in just such an empirical hand-to-mouth fashion. But it is wrong to present their legislation as if it marked a substantial shift from *laissez faire* to state intervention.

from *Disraeli* by R Blake (1966)

Q The same writer points to the balance that political circumstances required Disraeli to attempt in his formulation of Conservative policies

The truth is that Disraeli had principles when he led the party and believed in them sincerely, but they were not the 'principles', if that word can be used at all, of Young England. It is easy to underestimate Disraeli's innate Conservatism. He believed passionately in the greatness of England – not in itself a Tory monopoly. But he also believed no less deeply that England's greatness depended upon the ascendancy of the landed class. . . This does not mean that he wished to set class against class. On the contrary he proclaimed the doctrine of one nation and asserted that if the Conservative Party was not a national party it was nothing. But he did sincerely think that the nation would decline with the decline of the landed interest. Most of his specific attitudes can be traced to this sort of Conservatism: support of Crown, Church, Lords; dislike of Irish separatism with its threat to the land; anxiety to preserve the rule of the JPs in the counties; acceptance of cautious social reform in those geographical or metaphorical areas where the landed interest was least affected. Economic factors were soon to bring about the decline of the land more effectively than any political measures, and were indeed already doing so in his lifetime; but he did not live to see the full consequences.

The logic of the Conservative position after 1832 dictated the policy of accommodation with the business and commercial interests followed by Peel. The landed classes were on too narrow a political basis to rule alone. Disraeli, detesting Peel and devising a romantic but basically unrealistic Tory philosophy of his own, was responsible more than anyone else for the fall of Peel and the temporary repudiation of Peelism. He could not have done it single-handed, but without him it would probably not have been done at all. Yet when the dust settled, it became clear enough that, though Peel had fallen, the party was not going to get anywhere if it continued to repudiate Peelism. Disraeli saw this very early. He never abandoned or denied his own 'philosophy' but it had little effect on his actions – quite rightly, for no one in his senses would have tried to lead the Conservative Party after 1846 by reference to the principles of Young England. Disraeli's actual policy was essentially Peelite.

from *Disraeli* by R Blake (1966)

Questions

1 Explain the meaning of the following terms as they appear in Source D:

(*a*) 'hereditary coteries of exclusive nobles' (line 4) **(2 marks)**

(*b*) 'my Lord Derby and his colleagues have taken a happy opportunity to enlarge the privileges of the people of England' (lines 9–10) **(2 marks)**

2 Using your own knowledge, examine the political significance of the fears expressed by Salisbury in Source G. **(7 marks)**

3 In Sources D and H, Disraeli frequently uses the phrase 'the institutions of the country'. What did he mean by this? **(7 marks)**

4 How far can an understanding of Disraeli's Conservatism be drawn from Sources D and H? **(8 marks)**

5 How valuable to the historian is the analysis in Document I of the 1874 election results? **(9 marks)**

5 GLADSTONE AND LIBERALISM

It is an illustration of the lack of rigidity about British party political alignments in the first half of the century that Gladstone should have learned his Liberalism from Robert Peel, the Conservative Leader. The issue that obliged Gladstone to begin to move away from his earlier reactionary views was that of protection versus free trade. Gladstone's outstanding abilities and deep respect for Peel led to his being regarded as a natural successor to him. But with the break-up of the parties after 1846 Gladstone seemed uncertain as to where his political loyalties lay. He had developed a deep distaste for the two other major politicians of the time, Palmerston and Disraeli. An important experience that directed him towards Liberalism as an ideal was his witnessing of political oppression in Naples [A-D].

A vital stage in the turning of his Liberal ideas into practical policies came with his work as Chancellor of the Exchequer, first in Lord Aberdeen's Coalition Government (1852–55) and then in Palmerston's Whig-Liberal ministry (1859–65). His budgets of those years consolidated Britain's position as a free-trade nation and revolutionised the system of government finance [E-H].

Gladstone's first ministry, 1868–74, marked the 'High Tide of Liberalism', but it was not a period of unqualified success. Gladstone retired from the Party Leadership following the Liberal defeat in 1874. Two years later he re-entered the political arena in order to expose the Turkish atrocities in Bulgaria. This was the beginning of a major attack upon 'the evils of Beaconsfieldism', which culminated in his celebrated election campaign in the Midlothian constituency in 1879. Historians now consider that Midlothian marked a highly significant development in British politics [I-L].

Gladstone remained in politics for another fifteen years after his Midlothian victory, becoming Prime Minister on three occasions. The great issues that preoccupied his last years as a Liberal Statesman were the Eastern Question, Egypt, and, above all, Ireland [M].

A As a young man Gladstone had expressed his uncertainty concerning British political parties

Who may be right and who wrong in this fundamental principle lying at the root of party distinctions, is a deep and difficult question, and one in which we must perhaps rely mainly upon perceptions and persuasions incapable of analysis and ranking among the ultimate facts of our nature. The details of Revealed truth seem to me to bear out the choice which my mind has made: to indicate that we are as children and pupils, seeing in a glass darkly, appointed to self-government for the purpose of growth and strength, but not intended to regard it as an end valuable in itself: and as on the other hand necessary, but *less* necessary, than the counter-poising principle of obedience, while the two together as the active and the passive principle from the harmony of our nature.

from an unpublished essay by Gladstone, written in 1836

B Gladstone abandons protection
I learned the cause of the different trades out of the mouths of the deputations which were sent up to remit our proposals. So that by the close of the session I began really to know something about the matter and my faith in Protection except as a system of transition crumbled rapidly away.

From this time [1842] down to 1860 or thereabouts the question of Protection mainly determined the parliamentary history of the country and it became my fate to bear a very active part in it especially after the death of Sir Robert Peel. For my part I am a Free Trader on moral no less than on economic grounds: for I think human greed and selfishness are interwoven with every thread of the Protective system. In this great controversy Peel as I think displayed perfect honesty and inflexible courage. . . From the language he held to me in December 1845 I think he expected to carry the repeal of the Corn Law without breaking up his party. But meant at all hazards to carry it. A miscalculation followed which was more difficult in my opinion to explain. The opposition to the repeal depended chiefly on three men. The first was George Bentinck [a leader of the Young England movement], a man of iron will, whose whole soul was in the matter and whose convictions were profundly engaged. The next Lord Derby. He was a man brilliantly endowed: but his gifts of character were I think hardly equal to his talents. From the high position which he occupied he was a most ornamental leader. But he was not a man to fight doggedly for a losing cause. The third and not least remarkable was Disraeli. From first to last he simply played with the subject.

As long as George Bentinck lived, he was the animating principle of the Party: and he would certainly have urged it, I may say constrained it, to go all lengths for its purposes. But in 1848 he was removed by an early and sudden death. The change thus brought about was fundamental. The Protectionists were from thenceforth a house built upon the sand. Their leaders were two men, one of whom had no stomach for a desperate fight, while the other never dreamed of fighting at all, except for his career. Under these circumstances it was with astonishment that I listened to Peel when he said to me, 'I foresee that there will be a desperate struggle made for the restoration of Protection', and 'I think', he added, 'it will convulse the country'. Therefore in 1846–50 he made it the main principle of his parliamentary action to support the Whigs (without becoming himself a Whig or Liberal) and to keep out the Protectionists. I held this to be an hallucination. In my estimation Protection was certain to thrive and flourish so long as it continued irresponsible and could only be brought to its deserved extinction by being subjected to the touch of office, of governing the country, when as by the wand of a magician it would at once dissolve. Such was the issue to which it was brought in 1852: and the issue is before the world.

from Gladstone's *Protectionism 1840–60*, July 1894

C A modern biographer describes Gladstone's move towards Liberalism

[The] decade 1841–51 is the crucial period of his political development. In place of his earlier views he had developed a number of interests, which were not yet necessarily coherently interlocked but which, taken as a whole, made it increasingly difficult for him to co-operate with the Tory rump.

His aim had been not to reconstruct an abstract theory of the sort given in *The State in its Relations with the Church* [Gladstone's first book], but to arrive at a series of practical positions which would further national moral progress. He had developed a 'thorough Sir Robert Peel horror of *abstract* resolutions' and he never again attempted, as he had in his book, first to state an abstract principle, then to work it out in politics. Subsequently he invested practical measures with abstract principle; here lay one of the secrets of his great public success.

To say whether this constituted Liberalism is to measure him against an undefined standard. But it can be said that it placed him with the political economists on fiscal policy (Liberals to a man) – with the Whigs on civil liberties – with the Radicals . . . on colonial affairs, and – whether he liked it or not – with the moderates of European Liberalism on the Italian question. On the topics which had become central to his political interests, therefore, he found himself in each case allied with groups which, whatever they were, were not predominantly Tory. For a politician of Gladstone's type, the change in personal relationships follows the change of opinion. Of all the leading Peelites he had become the most Liberal, on many topics, in the sense of policy, but remained the most enthusiastic for a rejuvenated Conservative Party permeated and controlled by the Peelite group. 'Junction with the liberals' in 1852 would be 'our least natural position'; the function of the Peelites was 'working out a liberal policy through the medium of the Conservative party'. But in saying this, Gladstone already believed that in terms of issue and policy he would find great difficulty in supporting Derby's Conservative government at least until its protectionist proposals had been defeated.

from *Gladstone 1809–74* by H C G Matthew (1988)

D Gladstone reflects on the brotherhood of man

Had the case been one of illegality alone – had there been no other charge against the Government of Naples than that every day and in every act of its existence it breaks the fundamental law of the land, I for one should certainly have said whatever feelings we as Englishmen may entertain about such a state of things, it is not our business to rectify illegalities simply as such in other countries: we are not propagandists, we have no mission, we had better trust to the progress of events under the control of Providence to rectify this great evil.

But this illegality gross flagrant & univeral as it is becomes totally insignificant in comparison with the other features of this case; features which in my view convert every man into a Propagandist and give every man a mission, to expose if he cannot otherwise amend a gigantic iniquity such as has rarely in the history of man trampled upon Earth or lifted its audacious front to heaven.

There is a bond of flesh which unites man to man, there is a community of nature and of lot, of thought and feeling, of hope and aspiration, of weakness of sorrow and of suffering, which under certain rare circumstances obliges us with a power superior to that of ordinary rules of conduct ever framed with reference to the supposition of an average standard of behaviour among men, with certain limits of deviation this way and that. The present is one of these exceptional cases, for which no ordinary rules can provide.

from an entry for 13 February 1851 in *The Gladstone Diaries*

E Gladstone defines the purpose behind his budgets

To maintain a steady surplus of income over expenditure – to lower indirect taxes when excessive in amount for the relief of the people and bearing in mind the reproductive power inherent in such operations – to simplify our fiscal system by concentrating its pressure on a few well chosen articles of extended consumption – and to conciliate support to the Income Tax by marking its temporary character & by associating it with beneficial changes in the laws: these aims have been for fifteen years the labour of our life.

from a speech of Gladstone's in the House of Commons, 1857

F Gladstone at the Despatch box in the House of Commons

G The historical significance of Gladstone's work at the Exchequer

As chancellor, Gladstone compared himself to an architect altering a fine but decaying eighteenth-century mansion to a form fitted for the industrial age, designing the new building, controlling its construction, modifying its form as the years passed. Technically put, the function of the chancellor was to create a model of international free trade and then to interfere at the margin of the domestic economy on grounds of social justice:

'Once security has been taken that an entire society shall not be forced to pay an artificial price to some of its members for their production, we may safely commit the question (of cheapness of goods) to the action of competition among manufacturers, and of what we term the laws of supply and demand. As to the condition of the workpeople, experience has shown, especially in the case of the Factory Acts, that we should do wrong in laying down any abstract maxim as an invariable rule'.

from *Gladstone 1809–74* by H C G Matthew (1988)

H Gladstone's Liberalism at the time of his entering Palmerston's Government in 1859

To join the new administration, then, marked a party severance but no changed principles. I am far from denying the enormous significance of the party wrench, but it was not a conversion. Mr Gladstone was at this time in his politics a liberal reformer, a born lover of good government, of just practical laws, of wise improvement, of public business well handled, of a state that should emancipate and serve the individual. The necessity of summoning new driving force, and amending the machinery of the constitution, had not yet disclosed itself to him.

from *The Life of W E Gladstone* by J Morley (1903)

I A modern scholar reflects on the significance of Gladstone's first ministry

In terms of legislative achievement the government which Gladstone had now formed [1868] was to become one of the greatest of the nineteenth century and by far the most important of the four governments of which he was to be the head. If one wishes to define the substance of Gladstonian liberalism the actions of this government are much the best point of reference. Yet there was no plan in existence which might have charted the course this ministry was to take nor was it certain at the outset that its parliamentary majority would prove stable. The previous Parliament had been one of the least stable of the era since 1832 and it had come at the end of a twenty-year period of fluid party lines. There was no guarantee that Gladstone had been able to impose more than a temporary cohesion upon his followers through the Irish disestablishment policy. Disraeli had not abandoned hope that when this policy came to be put into legislative effect the Irish Church would be as damaging to Liberal unity as reform had been. In retrospect the first Gladstone government looks like the beginning of a new era of coherent political parties with a mass following in the country and of much else that was new and modern about the political system. Certain features of the situation were indeed novel and pointed to the future: Gladstone's role as a link between a parliamentary combination and a popular movement in the country, though Palmerston's role had not been so very different; the immediate resignation of Disraeli once the verdict of the country was clear; the Queen's summons to Gladstone, when perhaps only a few years previously she might in similar circumstances have first turned to Lord Russell or Lord Granville.

But in many other ways the novelty of the situation was not recognised, either by Gladstone or by others. He saw himself as the head of a parliamentary combination and the composition of his Cabinet reflected this. He was aware that many reforms were waiting to be taken up which had been in the air for a long time but had been held up in the days of Palmerston and had been impossible to proceed with in the unstable Parliament of 1865. Even the Conservative government had tried to do something about education; there was a royal commission sitting on the trade unions. His Cabinet colleagues were therefore bound to bring up schemes of various kinds and Gladstone would, once the Cabinet had collectively adopted them, facilitate their passage through Parliament. He personally, however, was above all concerned with his Irish crusade; his control over government policy as a whole was therefore not likely to be as complete as Peel's had been between 1841 and 1846.

from *Gladstone* by E J Feuchtwanger (1975)

J His biographer, John Morley, witnessed Gladstone's Midlothian election campaign in 1879

People came from the Hebrides to hear Mr Gladstone speak. Where there were six thousand seats, the applications were forty or fifty thousand. The weather was bitter and the hills were covered with snow, but this made no difference in cavalcades, processions, and the rest of the outdoor demonstrations. Over what a space had democracy travelled, and what a transition for its champion of the hour, since the days half a century back when the Christ Church undergraduate, the disciple of Burke and Canning, had ridden in anti-reform processions, been hustled by reform mobs, and had prayed for the blessing of heaven on the House of Lords for their honourable and manly decision in throwing out the bill. Yet the warmest opponent of popular government . . . might have found some balm for this extraordinary display of popular feeling, in the thought that it was a tribute to the most splendid political career of that generation; splendid in gifts and splendid in service, and that it was repaid, more-over, with none of the flattery associated with the name of demagogue. Mr Gladstone's counsels may have been wise or unwise, but the only flattery in the Midlothian speeches was the manly flattery contained in the fact that he took care to address all these multitudes of weavers, farmers, villagers, artisans, just as he would have addressed the House of Commons – with the same breadth and accuracy of knowledge, the same sincerity of interest, the same scruple in right reasoning, and the same appeal to the gravity and responsibility of public life. An aristocratic minister, speaking at Edinburgh soon after, estimated the number of words in Mr Gladstone's Midlothian speeches in 1879 at 85,840 and declared that his verbosity had become 'a positive danger to the commonwealth.' Tory critics solemnly declared that such per-formances were an innovation on the constitution, and aggravated the evil tendencies of democracy. Talk of this kind did not really impose for an instant on any man or woman of common sense. . .

It was the orator of concrete detail, of inductive instances, of energetic and immediate object; the orator confidently and by sure touch startling into watchfulness the whole spirit of civil duty in a man; elastic and supple, pressing fact and figure with a fervid insistence that was known from his career and character to be neither forced nor feigned, but to be himself. In a word, it was a man – a man impressing himself upon the kindled throngs by the breadth of his survey of great affairs of life and nations, by the depth of his vision, by the power of his stroke. Physical resources had much to do with the effect; his overflowing vivacity, the fine voice and flashing eye and a whole frame in free, ceaseless, natural and spontaneous motion. So he bore his hearers through long chains of strenuous periods, calling up by the marvellous transformations of his mien a strange succession of images – as if he were now a keen hunter, now some eager bird of prey, now a charioteer of fiery steeds kept well in hand, and now and again we seemed to hear the pity of dark wrath of a prophet, with the mighty rushing wind and the fire running along the ground.

All this was Mr Gladstone in Midlothian.

from *Life of Gladstone* by J Morley (1903)

K A modern estimate of the significance of the Midlothian campaign

In a carefully planned series of speeches Gladstone elaborated his indictment of the Conservative administration. The demagogic technique hinted at in Lancashire in1868 was now in full maturity. Traditionalists in both parties were disturbed in varying degrees by this tendency to shift the central focus of the political process from the chamber of the House to excited and roaring mass demonstrations.

Gladstone made of Midlothian a holy drama of politics, in which a small minority of those with the franchise acted as supers on the stage dominated by the protaganist, playing to an audience of the vast unenfranchised. Midlothian had more in common with a morality play, an Oberammergau Passion, than with a modern election. Being in Scotland, where constituencies were smaller, rather heightened this effect, already charged with associations of Sir Walter Scott. But the smallness of the constituency involved for Gladstone no inconsistency. He was appealing over the head of the classes to the virtuous masses; and his demand was essentially that the classes voting in Midlothian should vote in this sense as moral proxies to a higher electorate. The message of the morality play was of the 'evil instinct' which 'guided' the Conservatives in the 'choosing' of demoralising policies. Most emphasis was placed on foreign affairs. Gladstone summed up his message in 'six right principles' of foreign policy which would constitute the guidelines for Britain's international mission in the future: to foster the strength of the Empire by 'just legislation and economy at home' and to 'reserve the expenditure of that strength for great and worthy occasions abroad'; to defend the cause of peace; to strive to cultivate and maintain the concert of Europe; to 'avoid needless and entangling engagements' (this with the emphasis on selective intervention, for Cobdenite consumption); to acknowledge the equal rights of all nations; and to ensure that the foreign policy of England should be inspired always 'by the love of freedom'.

from *The Crisis of Imperialism, 1865–1915* by Richard Shannon (1974)

L Liberalism as popular politics

The Midlothian Campaign represented the flowering of a new style of politics, long in germination. As politics became more bureaucratised, extra-paliamentary speech-making provided the means of the Liberal intelligentsia to preserve its influence in British political life, and in doing so it linked the intellectual force of Liberal politics to a particular form of media-presentation. The full force of the popularisation of the Liberal ethos rose with the political press of the 1860s and died with it in the 1920s.

from H C G Matthew's introduction to the *Gladstone Diaries* (Vol IX, 1986)

M Gladstone reflects on the great issues of his last twenty years in politics

In the winter of 1873–4, the general election made necessary the retirement of the Ministry, of which I was then at the head. And I was most desirous of making their retirement the occasion of my own. I had served for more than forty years. And I felt myself to be in some measure out of touch with some of the tendencies of the Liberal party especially in religious matters. I thought they leant to the dethronement of the private conscience and to a generalised religion. I deeply desired an interval between Parliament and the grave, which might in the counsels of God be far or near. And in spite of the solicitations of my friends I persisted. For 1874, there was a sort of compromise 'without prejudice'. Having a title to some rest, I was not a very regular attendant but did not formally abdicate. When 1875 opened I carried the matter to issue and resigned the leadership, Hartington being chosen to fill the vacancy.

[The Eastern Question]

When in 1876 the Eastern question was pressed forward by the disturbances in the Turkish Empire, and especially by the cruel outrages in Bulgaria, I shrank naturally but perhaps unduly from recognising the claim they made upon me individually. I hoped that the Ministers would recognise the moral obligations to the subject races of the east, which we had in honour contracted as parties to the Crimean War, and to the Peace of Paris in 1856. I was slow to observe the real leanings of the Prime Minister, his strong sympathy with the Turk and his mastery in his own cabinet. I suffered others, Forster in particular, to go far ahead of me. At the close of the session a debate was raised upon the subject, and I had at length been compelled to perceive how the old idol was still to be worshipped at Constantinople, and that, as the only person surviving in the House of Commons who had been responsible for the Crimean war and the levelling of the bulwark raised by the treaty of Kainardji on behalf of the eastern Christians, I could no longer remain indifferent.

So I at once wrote and published on the Bulgarian case. It was with some difficulty on account of lumbago which made my body creak as I tried to write but at length I performed the task in bed with pillow props. From that time forward until the final consummation in 1879–80 I made the eastern question the main business of my life. I acted under a strong sense of individual duty without a thought of leadership: nevertheless it made me leader again whether I would or not. In 1880, Midlothian leading the way, the nation nobly answered to the call of justice and broadly recognised the brotherhood of man. It was the nation, not the classes.

[Egypt, Afghanistan, South Africa]

Thus it came about that I was fastened down to the resumption of the Premiership in 1880, and I learned in a practical way how difficult a thing it is to retire when by long use a man has become an acknowledged and prominent figure on the public stage.

During the first two years of that Government we had accomplished important purposes in Afghanistan, in South Africa, in the application of the Treaty of Berlin, and in the rectification of finance. The Egyptian entanglement had begun but we did not yet know how serious it would prove. There had however risen from the ground to confront us another formidable figure of which in 1880 we hardly dreamed – the Irish question; and it assumed such grave dimensions that although the engagements of 1880 were fulfilled I found that new ties had been woven around me which absolutely precluded my retirement.

[Ireland]

The Irish question lay so near the very heart of the Empire that no claim which it legitimately made could on any account be disregarded. We went or tried to go to the bottom of it in the Land Act of 1881, only to discover that we had not reached the core and the national aspiration was that which really required from us and from the country an Aye or a No. At the outset of 1882 I had spoken on the principle. By the Franchise Act of 1884–5 we made a long step towards the solution, for we put the Irish people, virtually the whole Irish people, to speak its mind. That mind was spoken plainly enough at the general election of 1885: and it also soon appeared that the Irish demand was capable of being bounded by the limits required under the constitution of the United Kingdom. I could not but entertain some belief in the reality of the manifestations amounting to promises which the Tory Government had held out to the Irish party. And I took the daring step, only to be justified by the circumstances of the case, if justified at all, of making known to an adverse Government my readiness to give all the aid in my power for the settlement of the Irish question. Thus opened the new drama. For another seven years from 1885 to 1892 we fought a national and popular battle – resembling that of 1876 to 1880 for the subject races of the east. And we were probably on the way to a result not less decisive, when the deplorable disclosures in the case of Mr Parnell introduced discord into the Irish ranks and not only diminished the numerical power and broke up the united vote of nationalism in

Ireland, but naturally presented to the British mind an altered view and kept our majority within bounds such as not to abash the courage or audacity of the House of Lords.

from W E Gladstone's *Autobiographica* (July 1894)

Questions

1 From the evidence in Sources B, C and D, suggest reasons why Gladstone came later to modify the views he had earlier expressed in Source A. **(7 marks)**

2 Using your own knowledge, and the evidence in Sources E, G and H, evaluate the importance of Gladstone's work as Chancellor of the Exchequer in the development of his Liberalism. **(8 marks)**

3 How far does the argument advanced in Source I support the idea that Gladstone's ministry of 1868–74 marked 'the high tide of Liberalism'? **(7 marks)**

4 Is there any major difference between the views of Gladstone's contemporary biographer, Morley (Source J), and those of his modern biographers, Shannon and Matthew (Sources K and L), regarding the place of the Midlothian campaign in the growth of Gladstone's Liberalism? **(8 marks)**

5 In the light of his analysis in Source M, how accurate is it to say that after 1874 Gladstone's Liberalism became a matter not of party politics but of moral issues? **(10 marks)**

6 DISRAELI AND IMPERIALISM

Disraeli did not become an advocate of Imperialism until quite late in his career. In his earlier days he had described Britain's overseas colonies as 'millstones round our necks'. The first clear intimation of what was to become a deep commitment to British Imperialism was contained in a speech he made in 1857 at the time of the Indian mutiny [A]. What led Disraeli to adopt Imperialism as a fundamental aspect of Conservatism was Gladstone's hostility to any form of foreign commitment. Disraeli judged that the idea of British greatness, expressed through imperial expansion, would prove a vote-winner with the growing electorate. He publicised the new Conservative attitude towards Empire in a series of powerful speeches in the early 1870s. It was part of his campaign to convince the voters that Gladstone's reforming Liberal Government was engaged in destroying the nation's true strength and character [B].

There are four distinct episodes which illustrate Disraeli's Imperialism in action:

(a)   The Suez Canal Shares

When in 1875 the bankrupt Khedive of Egypt appeared willing to sell his holdings in the Suez Canal project, currently being constructed under the direction of the French engineer, De Lesseps, Disraeli acted opportunely and speedily [C-G].

(b)   The Declaration of the Queen as Empress of India

The Royal Titles Act of 1876 was the logical fulfilment of Disraeli's wish to make his Sovereign the personification of the imperial idea [H-I].

(c)   The Afghan War

Disraeli's determination to resist any challenge to Britain's position in India, 'The Jewel in the Crown', was evident in his policy over Afghanistan. Russia's nineteenth-century expansion into Asia appeared by the late 1870s directly to threaten India. In Disraeli's judgement, it was necessary for Britain to take control of Afghanistan, India's north-western neighbour, as a buffer state. Lord Lytton, Britain's Vice-Roy in India, was encouraged to take a firm line with the Amir (ruler), Sher Ali, of Afghanistan and oblige him to reject Russian overtures and accept British authority. When the Amir resisted a British army was sent to Afghanistan [J-O].

(d)   The Zulu War
In 1876, Disraeli despatched a British army to the Transvaal in support
of the Dutch Boers in their war with the native Zulus. His intention was
not primarily to aid the Boers but to assert British authority in Southern
Africa. Things went badly at first, the Zulus inflicting a major defeat
on the British forces at Isandhlwana in 1879 before being finally
overcome later that same year at Ulundi [P-T].

A Disraeli on Anglo-Indian relations after the mutiny
I think that the great body of the population of that country [India]
ought to know that there is for them a future of hope. I think we
ought to temper justice with mercy – justice the most severe with
mercy the most indulgent.

The course which I recommend is this: You ought at once, whether
you receive news of success or defeat, to tell the people of India that
the relation between them and their real Ruler and Sovereign, Queen
Victoria, shall be drawn nearer. You must act upon the opinion of
India on that subject immediately and you can only act upon the
opinion of Eastern nations through their imagination. You ought to
have a Royal Commission sent by the Queen from this country to
India immediately to inquire into the grievances of the various classes
of that population. You ought to issue a royal proclamation to the
people of India declaring that the Queen of England is not a Sovereign
who will countenance the violation of treaties; that the Queen of
England is not a Sovereign who will disturb the settlement of
property; that the Queen of England is a Sovereign who will respect
their laws, their usages, their customs and, above all, their religion.
Do this, and do it not in corner, but in a model and manner which
will attract universal attention and excite the general hope of
Hindustan, and you will do as much as all your fleets and armies can
achieve.

from a speech in the House of Commons, 1857

B Disraeli's justification of Imperialism
If you look at the history of this country since the advent of Liberalism
– forty years ago – you will find that there has been no effort so
continuous, so subtle, supported by so much energy, and carried on
with so much ability and acumen, as the attempts of Liberalism to
effect the disintegration of the Empire of England. And, gentlemen,
of all its efforts, this is the one which has been the nearest to success.
It has been shown with precise, with mathematical demonstration,
that there never was a jewel in the Crown of England that was so
truly costly as the possession of India. How often has it been

suggested that we should at once emancipate ourselves from this costly incubus. Well, that result was nearly accomplished. When those subtle views were adopted by the country under the plausible plea of granting self-government to the Colonies, I confess that I myself thought that the tie was broken. Not that I for one object to self-government; I cannot conceive how our distant colonies can have their affairs administered except by self-government. But self-government, in my opinion, when it was conceded, ought to have been conceded as part of a great policy of Imperial consolidation. It ought to have been accompanied by an Imperial tariff, by securities for the people of England for the enjoyment of the un-appropriated lands which belong to the Sovereign as trustee, and by a military code which should have precisely defined the means and the responsibilities by which the Colonies should be defended, and by which, if necessary, this county should call for aid from the colonies themselves. It ought, further, to have been accompanied by the institution of some representative council which would have brought the colonies into constant relation with the Home Government.

adapted from Disraeli's speech at the Crystal Palace in 1872

C Disraeli to Queen Victoria
18 November 1875
The Khedive, on the eve of bankruptcy, appears desirous of parting with his shares in the Suez Canal and has communicated, confidentially, with General Stanton. There is a French company in negotiation with His Highness, but they propose only to make an advance with complicated stipulations.

'Tis an affair of millions; about four at least; but would give the possessor an immense, not to say preponderating, influence in the management of the Canal.

It is vital to your Majesty's authority and power at this critical moment, that the Canal should belong to England, and I was so decided and absolute with Lord Derby on this head, that he ultimately adopted my views and brought the matter before the Cabinet yesterday. The Cabinet was unanimous in their decision, that the interest of the Khedive should, if possible, be obtained, and we telegraphed accordingly.

Last night, there was another telegram from General Stanton which indicated some new difficulties, but the Cabinet meets again to-day (at two o'clock) and we shall consider them.

The Khedive now says, that it is absolutely necessary that he should have between three and four millions sterling by the 30th of this month!

Scarcely breathing time! But the thing must be done.

D Disraeli to the Queen
19 November 1875
The Cabinet considered the affairs of the Khedive yesterday for one hour and a half.

The pecuniary embarrassments of the Khedive appear to be very serious, and it is doubtful whether a financial catastrophe can be avoided. The business is difficult, but it is as important as difficult, and must not be relinquished. We received telegrams from General Stanton, who had personally seen the Khedive, and we also returned telegrams.

The Khedive voluntarily pledged himself, that, whatever happened, your Majesty's government should have the refusal of his interest in the Canal. All that can be done now, is to keep the business well in hand.

E The Queen to Disraeli
19 November 1875
The Queen thanks Mr Disraeli for his letters. She has telegraphed her approval of the course he intends pursuing respecting the Suez Canal, but fears it will be difficult to arrange.

F Disraeli to the Queen
24 November 1875
It is just settled: you have it, Madam; the French Government has been out-generaled. They tried too much, offering loans at an usurious rate, and with conditions, which would have virtually given them the government of Egypt.

The Khedive, in despair and disgust, offered your Majesty's government to purchase his shares outright. He never would listen to such a proposition before.

Four million sterling! and almost immediately. There was only one firm that could do it – Rothschilds. They behaved admirably; advanced the money at a low rate, and the entire interest of the Khedive is now yours, Madam.

Yesterday the Cabinet sat for 7 hours and more on this, and Mr Disraeli has not had one moment's rest to-day; therefore this despatch must be pardoned, as his head is rather weak. He will tell the whole wondrous tale tomorrow.

He was in Cabinet to-day, when your Majesty's second telegram arrived, which must be his excuse for his brief and stupid answer: but it was 'the crisis.'

G Disraeli to Lady Bradford
25 November 1875
I will now tell you a great State secret, certainly the most important of this year, and not one of the least events of our generation.

After a fortnight of the most unceasing labour and anxiety, I (for between ourselves, and ourselves only, I may be egotistical in this matter) I have purchased for England the Khedive of Egypt's interest in the Suez Canal.

We have had all the gamblers, capitalists, financiers of the world, organised and platooned in bands of plunderers, arrayed against us, and secret emissaries in every corner, and have baffled them all, and have never been suspected. The day before yesterday, Lesseps, whose company has the remaining shares, backed by French Government, whose agent he was, made a great offer. Had it succeeded, the whole of the Suez Canal would have belonged to France, and they might have shut it up!

H The Queen becomes Empress

The population of India is not the population it was when we carried the Bill of 1858. There has been a great change in the habits of the people. That which the press could not do, that which our influence had failed in doing, the introduction of railroads has done; and the people of India move about in a manner which could never have been anticipated, and are influenced by ideas and knowledge which never before reached or touched them. What was the gossip of bazaars is now the conversation of villages. You think they are unaware that Tartary, that great conquering power of former times, is now at last conquered? No; not only do they know what has occurred, not only are they well acquainted with the power which has accomplished this great change, but they know well the title of the great Prince who has brought about so wonderful a revolution. I have listened with surprise night after night to hon. gentlemen, on both sides of the House, translating the title of Empress into all sorts of languages, and indicating to us what name would at last be adopted. The nations and populations that can pronounce the word Emperor, and that habitually use it, will not be slow to accept the title of Empress. That is the word which will be adopted by the nations and populations of India; and in announcing, as Her Majesty will do by proclamation, that she adopts that title, confidence will be given to her Empire in that part of the world, and it will be spoken, in language which cannot be mistaken, that the Parliament of England have resolved to uphold the Empire of India.

from Disraeli's speech in the House of Commons, 1876

1 'New Crowns for Old Ones': Punch cartoon, 1876

J Disraeli to Lady Bradford
28 December 1878
On Monday I go to Windsor to dine with the Empress of India. It is
New Year's Day, when she is proclaimed in Hindustan, and she wishes
the day to be celebrated, and 'marked' hereafter. The Faery is much
excited about the doings at Delhi. They have produced great effect
in India, and indeed throughout the world, and vindicate triumphantly
the policy of the measure which was so virulently, but so fruitlessly,
opposed. It has no doubt consolidated our empire there. Our poetical
Viceroy is doing justice to the occasion. The Faery is so full of the
great incident, and feels everything about it so keenly that she sent
me a Xmas card and signed her good wishes *VICTORIA REGINA et
IMPERATRIX* [Queen and Empress].

K Disraeli to Lord Cranbrook (Secretary for India)
September 1878
I am convinced the country requires that we shall act with decision
and firmness on this Afghan question. So far as I can judge, the
feeling is strong, and rising, in the country. So long as they thought
there was 'Peace with Honour' the conduct of the Government was
popular, but if they find there is no peace, they will soon be apt to
conclude there is also no honour.

With Lytton's general policy I entirely agree. I have always been
opposed to, and deplored, 'masterly inactivity.'

No doubt Salisbury's views, [Foreign Secretary] under ordinary
circumstances, would be prudent; but there are occasions when
prudence is not wisdom. And this is one. There are times for action.
We must control, and even create events.

No doubt our Envoy will make the best terms he can. He will, of
course, not show all his cards at once, but I am clearly of the opinion
that what we want, at this present moment, is to prove our ascendancy
in Afghanistan and to accomplish that, we must not stick at trifles.

L Disraeli to the Duke of Richmond, October 1878
To call the Cabinet together would agitate all Europe, and I should
think the Vice-Roy was quite prepared for the probable incident that
has occurred. I telegraphed yesterday, but I have not yet an answer.
It is unfortunate, at such a moment, that the Secretary for Foreign
Affairs should be at Dieppe and Secretary for India at Balmoral. We
are terribly scattered; naturally in Sept., but events happen every
day. They have no recess and no holidays. I think with firmness we
shall settle all the other things and this too.

M Disraeli to Lord Salisbury

October 1878

I have been obliged to summon the Cabinet. I found they were talking
all sorts of nonsense over the country; especially some in whose
prudence I still had some lingering trust; and there were already 'two
parties in the Cabinet,' and all that.

I have given the deepest attention and study to the situation and
read with becoming consideration all Lytton's wonderful pamphlets;
which are admirable both in their grasp and their detail; and this is
my opinion. His policy is perfectly fitted to a state of affairs in which
Russia was our assailant; But Russia is not our assailant. She has
sneaked out of her hostile position, with sincerity in my mind, but
scarcely with dignity, and if Lytton had only been quiet and obeyed
my orders, I have no doubt that, under the advice of Russia, Sher Ali
would have been equally prudent.

N Disraeli argues for secure borders

Our north-western frontier is a haphazard and not a scientific frontier.
It is in the power of any foe so to embarrass and disturb our dominion
that we should be obliged to maintain the presence of a great military
force in that quarter, entailing on the country a proportionate
expenditure. These are unquestionably great evils, and former
Viceroys have had their attention called with anxiety to the state of
our frontier. Recently, however, some peculiar circumstances have
occurred in that part of the world, which have convinced Her
Majesty's government that the time has arrived when we must
terminate all this inconvenience and prevent all this possible injury.
With this view we have made arrangements by which, when
completed, in all probability at no distant day, all anxiety respecting
the north-western frontier of India will be removed.

from Disraeli's speech in the House of Lords, November 1878

O Disraeli as nationalist

I know there are some who think that the power of England is on the
wane. We have been informed lately that ours will be the lot of Genoa
and Venice and Holland. But, my Lord Mayor, there is a great
difference between the condition of England and those picturesque
and interesting communities. We have, during ages of prosperity,
created a nation of 34,000,000; a nation who are enjoying, and have
long enjoyed, the two greatest blessings of civil life – justice and
liberty. A nation of that character is more calculated to create empires
than to give them up; and I feel confident, if England is true to herself,
if the English people prove themselves worthy of their ancestors, if
they possess still the courage and determination of their forefathers,

their honour will never be tarnished and their power will never diminish.

from Disraeli's speech at the Guildhall, 1878

P Disraeli to the Queen
December 1878
Lord Beaconsfield with his humble duty to your Majesty, must offer his congratulations to his beloved Sovereign, on the signal triumph of your Majesty's arms. The letter of the Amir, which Lord Beaconsfield underlined some days ago, in a telegram which he forwarded to your Majesty, has just been received by the Secretary of State, and it is clear we may demand any terms we like. Of course, he offers to receive your Majesty's Envoy at Kabul.

The check to Russia, to use a very mild expression, is complete. Lord Beaconsfield has no doubt, that expectations were held out by Russia of military aid to the Amir.

Lord Beaconsfield has summoned the Cabinet to meet at three o'clock to-day, to consider the Amir's letter, and the situation generally. The debates proved last night that the Opposition is broke into pieces on the great question of the war. They dare not face it, but take refuge in mere squabbling about sentences in despatches. Lord Beaconsfield closed the debate in the House of Lords to his satisfaction, and is not worse for what was a considerable, tho' not very prolonged, physical exertion. He hopes your Majesty is well on this bright morning, which is as bright as your Majesty's imperial fortunes.

Q Lord Carnarvon [Colonial Secretary] to Disraeli
September/October 1876
Matters at the Cape are extremely critical. They need very prompt handling. The Dutch army is apparently in extremis, and I have received information that a meeting has already been called by a certain part of the people to ask for our intervention and to take over the Govt. of the country. Some even of the Dutch authorities appear to be consenting parties.

It is on every ground of the highest importance not to lose this opportunity, and I propose to send out by the mail of Friday, Sir Theophilus Shepstone, the man who has the most intimate knowledge of South African affairs and the greatest influence alike over natives and Dutch – with a secret despatch empowering him to take over the Transvaal government and country, and to become the first English Governor.

October 1876
The progress of events in S Africa seems to bring a possible

annexation of the Transvaal Republic and the consequent confederation of the various colonies and states within sight. Much, however, will depend upon every preparation being now made to enable us to take advantage of the feeling of the time.

Under these circumstances I am preparing a permissive Bill to allow these colonies and states to confederate. My next step must be, without loss of time, to bring S African opinion to bear upon it in such a way as to secure some criticism and expression of feeling on it. If this is, as I hope, favourable, there will be no difficulty in passing the measure through Parliament.

R Sir Michael Hicks Beach [Colonial Secretary] to Disraeli
January 1879

There is, I hope, a good prospect of the war being short and successful, like the Afghan campaign. The reinforcements would arrive just about in time to take part in it; Frere [special Envoy] seemed, from the last letters I have received, very confident, though these letters were written at a time when they thought no reinforcements were coming; the Zulus are reported to be much divided in opinion, likely to be rendered more so by some of the demands which Frere has made, so that Cetywayo's [Zulu Chief] position may be very similar to that of Sher Ali; and the Boers, who might place us in a very difficult situation by rising in the Transvaal while we are engaged with the Zulus, are said to be perfectly passive, according to their nature, waiting to see what will turn up. When the Zulus have submitted or are beaten, the Boers will be afraid to move.

S Disraeli to the Queen
February 1879

Lord Beaconsfield with his humble duty to your Majesty. It has been a very agitating day with this terrible news from South Africa, which to Lord Beaconsfield is very unintelligible. The Cabinet met, and have sent five regiments of Infantry instead of three asked for by Lord Chelmsford, and all the Cavalry and Artillery and stores which he requested. It is to be hoped, that, he may be equal to the occasion, but it is impossible not to feel that this disaster has occurred to the Headquarters column, which he was himself commanding. This sad news has come when, by indefatigable efforts, everything was beginning to look bright. It will change everything, reduce our Continental influence and embarrass our finances.

T The Queen to Disraeli
February 1879

[Lord Beaconsfield] must not be downhearted for a moment, but show a bold front to the world. This ought, however, to be a lesson never to reduce our forces, which was just going to be done; for, with our enormous Empire, we must always be prepared for such contingencies.

U Disraeli to the Queen
July 1879

The disturbance in our councils was occasioned by the unexpected exposition of the expenditure of the Zulu War, and of the ways and means proposed to provide for it by the Chancellor the Exchequer. It seems that the immediate expenditure has not been less that five millions and further demands are anticipated; of this little sum more that a million and a half have been provided by the House of Commons and this was borrowed. The Chancellor of the Exchequer said, that he could not propose to borrow any more, and that the balance must be supplied by taxation; and as an increased income tax had supplied our previous military expenditure he proposed now to have recourse to a considerable increase of the duties on tea.

It is impossible to name a tax more unpopular. Tea is an article which, above all others, has entered into the life of the people. They have introduced it into the principal meal – their dinner. Its consumption is the basis of the great Temperance movement. The Cabinet was alarmed and its principal members were the strongest in their comments.

We are placed in this painful position by a war, which, if not in time unnecessary, was unwisely precipitated, weakening us thereby in our settlement of the Levant [the Near East], and which, but for singular energy, would have embarrassed us in the arrangement of our Indian frontier – a war, which, had we had the prudence to prepare the indispensable transport before we declared it, might have been concluded in a month, nor required more than two or three thousand men.

Questions

1 According to the evidence in Source B what had led Disraeli to change his original attitude towards the colonies, as expressed in Source A? **(7 marks)**

2 By reference to the correspondence recorded in Sources C–G, trace the steps by which Disraeli acquired the Suez Canal for Britain.
(8 marks)

3 Of what value to the historian are Sources H and J as illustrations of Disraeli's concept of imperialism? **(7 marks)**

4 Drawing on your own knowledge and the evidence provided by

Sources K–P, examine the contention that Disraeli's policy towards Afghanistan was determined solely by his fear of Russia. **(9 marks)**

5 Does the evidence in Sources Q–U support or contradict the view that in all essentials Disraeli's attitude towards South Africa was the same as his attitude towards India? **(9 marks)**

7 GLADSTONE AND IRELAND

Gladstone's policy towards Ireland, the issue which dominated the last twenty-five years of his career, is a vital aspect of his Liberalism. In 1868, on becoming Prime Minister for the first time, he pledged himself to the solution of the Irish problem. Nowhere had that problem been better defined than in Disraeli's analysis of 1844 [A].

In 1868 Gladstone announced that he was taking up the Irish question in the name of 'The God of Truth and Justice'. He had earlier declared that he was prepared 'to lead the Liberal Party to martyrdom' over Ireland [B]. Gladstone used the metaphor of the mythical poison-bearing Upas tree to define Ireland's three basic problems. Identifying the three poisonous branches as the land question, education and the Irish Church, Gladstone committed himself to lopping them off by means of legislation. His first move was to disestablish the Anglican Church in Ireland [C-D]. Turning to the land question, Gladstone in 1870 introduced a Bill intended to protect Irish tenants against arbitrary eviction [E].

Gladstone's attempt to chop off the third branch of the Upas tree took the form of the Irish University Bill of 1873. Recognising that the provision of higher education for Irish Catholics was 'scandalously bad', this measure aimed to create a new university in Dublin which would be open to Catholics and would be on a par with the existing Trinity College that traditionally catered for Protestants. The Bill foundered on Catholic opposition to its clauses prohibiting the teaching of Theology [G].

In a further attempt to ease the troubled situation in Ireland Gladstone took the bold step of proposing to the Queen that the Prince of Wales might be usefully employed as resident Viceroy in Ireland [H]. The Queen was not amused and let her annoyance be known by strongly hinting that Gladstone should not interfere in matters that did not concern him.

When Gladstone returned to office in 1880 the situation in Ireland was even more threatening. The bitterness of the native Irish had, if anything, increased. Government coercion and Fenian (extreme Irish Nationalist) terrorism had created greater Anglo-Irish hostility [I]. Conscious that his 1870 Irish Land Act had failed to give Irish tenants the protection he had sought, Gladstone introduced a second Land Act in 1881. It aimed to establish the 'Three Fs' – fair rents, fixity of tenure, free sale [J].

Organised by C.S. Parnell, the Leader of the Irish Land League, the Irish MPs in Westminster interpreted each of Gladstone's attempted reforms as concessions forced out of a reluctant Government. They resolved to obstruct Government and Parliament at every turn. In 1881 Parnell was arrested and held in Kilmainham Gaol, Dublin, on charges of seditious conspiracy. Gladstone was not against coercion, but he preferred conciliation and accepted the offer of Joseph Chamberlain, the leading radical in the Liberal Party, to negotiate some form of unofficial agreement with Parnell, whereby the Irish Leader would use his influence to lessen the violence in Ireland. This move became known as the 'Kilmainham Treaty' [K].

Gladstone suffered a considerable personal tragedy when his nephew, Lord Frederick Cavendish, whom he had sent to Dublin as the new Irish Secretary, was murdered in Phoenix Park [M]. Despite such tragedies Gladstone was beginning to move towards the idea that reform was not enough, that only a political settlement could solve Ireland's problems [L–O].

Knowing that Home Rule would be acceptable to neither the Hartington Whigs on the right of the Liberal Party nor the Chamberlain Radicals on the left, Gladstone originally hoped that there could be a joint Liberal-Conservative introduction of such a measure. He was also willing to support the Conservatives if they chose to introduce it as their own answer to the Irish Question. His plans were destroyed by his son, Herbert's, unintentional leaking to the press that his father was a convert to Home Rule. Salisbury and the Conservative Party considered that this revelation relieved them of the responsibility for tackling Ireland. They handed the 'poisoned chalice' back to Gladstone [P]. Gladstone was well aware that the greatest barrier to Home Rule was the Ulster Question. It was in defence of the right of Protestant Ulster to remain part of the United Kingdom that at this juncture turned the overwhelming majority of the Conservative Party and some Liberals into 'Unionists' [Q]. Despite the power of his parliamentary performance, the Home Rule Bill was defeated on its second reading, over ninety Liberals voting with the Conservatives against it. This marked an irreparable division in the Liberal Party.

Undeterred by the failure of the Bill, Gladstone remained dedicated to the eventual implementation of Home Rule. He calculated that with the support of the Irish Nationalist MPs, who held the balance between the Liberals and the Conservative-Unionists in the Commons, it might still be achieved. What weakened his position was the undermining of the authority of Parnell as Leader of the Irish Party by his involvement in 1890 in a divorce scandal [R].

In 1893, during his fourth and last administration (1892–94), Gladstone introduced a second Home Rule Bill. It passed successfully, if narrowly, through the Commons, but was rejected by the House of Lords. This defeat occasioned his last speech in the Commons, a bitter attack on the power of the unelected Upper Chamber to thwart the will of the democratic assembly [S].

A The Irish question defined

[A] dense population in extreme distress inhabits an island where there is an Established Church which is not their Church, and a territorial aristocracy, the richest of whom live in distant capitals. Thus you have a starving population, an absentee aristocracy, and an alien Church, and in addition the weakest executive in the world. That is the Irish question.

from Disraeli's speech in the House of Commons, 1844

B Gladstone expresses the depth of his commitment to Ireland

We have now to deal with the . . . Irish question, and the Irish question is in a category by itself. It would be almost a crime in a minister to omit anything that might serve to mark, and bring home to the minds of men, the gravity of the occasion. Moreover, I am persuaded that the Queen's own sympathies would be, not as last year, but in the same current as ours. To this great country the state of Ireland after seven hundred years of our tutelage is, in my opinion, so long as it continues, an intolerable disgrace, and a danger so absolutely transcending all others, that I call it the only real danger of the noble empire of the Queen.

Gladstone to Lord Granville, January 1870

C Gladstone likens the Irish Church to

. . . some tall tree of noxious growth, lifting its head to Heaven and poisoning the atmosphere of the land as far as its shadow can extend. It is still there, gentlemen, but now at last the day has come when, as we hope, the axe has been laid to the root [*loud cheers*]. . . There lacks, gentlemen, but one stroke more – the stroke of these Elections [*loud cheers*]. It will then, once and for all, topple to its fall and on that day the heart of Ireland will leap for joy, and the mind and conscience of England and Scotland will repose with thankful satisfaction upon the thought that something has been done towards the discharge of national duty, and towards deepening and widening the foundations of public strength, security and peace. [*loud and prolonged applause.*]

from an election speech of Gladstone's, October 1868

D Gladstone justifies the disestablishment Bill to the Commons

In the removal of this establishment I see the discharge of a debt of civil justice, the disappearance of a national, almost a world-wide

E Gladstone, the champion of Ireland

reproach, a condition indispensable to the success of every effort to secure the peace and contentment of that country; finally relief to a devoted clergy from a false position, cramped and beset by hopeless prejudice, and the opening of a freer career to their sacred ministry.

from a speech in March 1869

F Gladstone explains the purpose of the Irish Land Act of 1870
The object the Government have in a view is to give, to the occupiers of the soil in Ireland, that sense of security which they require in order to pursue their calling with full advantage to the community and to themselves, and to do this in such a way as to create the smallest possible disturbance to existing arrangements, and to preserve, it might almost be said, to restore, the essential rights of property. The most essential provisions of the Bill in this view will be:

1. To confirm by law the custom called the Ulster Custom.

2. To provide for the occupier disturbed by the act of his landlord, where that custom does not prevail, a just compensation on losing his holding, either to be measured by other prevailing usages, or according to a scale set out in the Act, in consideration of the serious injury done to him, under the circumstances of that country, by the loss of his means of employment.

3. But to provide that by giving leases of an adequate length landlords may relieve themselves from the obligation to give compensation on this basis.

4. To lay down the principle that improvements in agricultural holdings effected by the tenant are to be henceforward presumed to be his property.

5. To create a judicial authority in Ireland which is to apply the provisions of the new law.

Gladstone to the Queen, January 1870

G Opposition to the Irish University Bill
Strange to say, it is the opposition of the Roman Catholic bishops that brings about the present difficulty; and this although they have not declared an opposition to the Bill outright, but have wound up their list of objections with a resolution to present petitions praying for its amendment. Still their attitude of what may be called growing hostility has had these important rules. Firstly, it has deadened that general willingness of the Liberal Party, which the measure itself had created, to look favourably on a plan such as they might hope would obtain acquiescence, and bring about contentment. Secondly, the

great majority of the bishops are even more hostile than the resolutions, which were apparently somewhat softened as the price of unanimity; and all *these* bishops, working upon Liberal Irish members through their political interest in their seats, have proceeded so far that from twenty to twenty-five may go against the Bill, and as many may stay away. When to these are added the small knot of discontented Liberals and mere fanatics which so large a party commonly contains, the government majority, now taken at only 85, disappears.

Gladstone to the Queen, March 1873

H Gladstone proposes that the Prince of Wales be Irish Viceroy

Whether His Royal Highness would consent to enter into this design, is a matter which Mr Gladstone's duty would not allow him to consider or to open, until it had been submitted to Your Majesty. Whether it would, if attempted, be found suitable for him, Mr Gladstone must not presume too confidently to pronounce. Yet he will venture to express an opinion that the admirable social qualities and the activity of the Prince would find in it a field for most beneficial exercise; and that an introduction to public business, which will in the course of nature at some period make large and weighty demands upon him, would here, and cannot elsewhere be supplied in a form at once effectual and unpresuming. Speaking humbly for himself, Mr Gladstone believes that the plan would draw out in the Prince's character what has hitherto had no adequate opportunity either of manifestation or of growth. But, even if the very worst came to the very worst, and total failure were the result, the experiment, if such it is to be called, need not be persisted in; the provision for the government of Ireland would remain complete; only it would have undergone an improvement.

Gladstone to the Queen, July 1872

I A leading Irish MP describes Gladstone's dilemma

The Irish peasant classes were in despair. Agrarian outrage became frequent in Ireland, and Mr Gladstone's Government believed it necessary to adopt new coercive legislation. The whole thing had got into the old vicious circle again. The legislative refusal of the tenants' rights caused agrarian disturbance, agrarian disturbance gave an occasion for coercion, further coercion led only to new disturbance ... I remember speaking in the House of Commons some time during the earlier period of Mr Gladstone's administration, and declaring my conviction that the action of the House of Lords in rejecting the Compensation for Disturbance Bill was the fountain and origin of all the agrarian trouble then going on in Ireland. I shall never forget how Mr Gladstone, seated on the Treasury bench, leaning across the table, with flashing eyes and earnest gestures, called 'Hear! Hear! Hear!' to my declaration. Mr Gladstone was between two terrible difficulties at the time, the difficulty with the House of Lords and the difficulty with the Irish people. The Irish peasantry are a very intelligent peasantry. They saw that the House of Lords had strength enough to reject Mr Gladstone's small and temporary measure, and they asked what chance was there for the passing of his scheme of permanent land reform. Over and over again has a tenant-farmer said to me: we don't blame Mr Gladstone; but we know only too well that the House of Lords will never let him do anything for the good of Ireland. So there grew up in the minds and hearts of the Irish people a feeling of utter disbelief that anything good could ever come for them out of even the best-intentioned English statesmanship. Agrarian outrages are, under such conditions, the natural, the inevitable result of popular despair.

from *The Story of Gladstone's Life* by Justin McCarthy (1898)

J The 'Three F's' of 1881
On the morning that this Bill passes every landlord and tenant will be subject to certain new provisions of the law of great importance. In the first place, an increase of rent will be restrained by certain rules. In the second place, the compensation for disturbance will be regulated according to different rates. And in the third place – more important probably than any – the right to sell the tenant's interest will be universally established. These are some of the means outside the Court which we propose; but there will also remain to the tenant the full power of going to the Court to fix a judicial rent, which may be followed by judicial tenant right. The judicial rent will entail a statutory term of 15 years. . . Evictions will hereafter, we trust, be only for default.

from Gladstone's speech in the Commons, April 1881

K The 'Kilmainham Treaty'
The cabinet are of opinion that the time has now arrived when with a view to the interests of law and order in Ireland, the three members of parliament who have been imprisoned on suspicion since last October, should be immediately released; and that the list of suspects should be examined with a view to the release of all persons not believed to be associated with crimes. They propose at once to announce to parliament their intention to propose, as soon as necessary business will permit, a Bill to strengthen the ordinary law in Ireland for the security of life and property, while reserving their

discretion with regard to the Life and Property Protection Act (of 1881) which however, they do not at present think it will be possible to renew, if a favourable state of affairs shall prevail in Ireland.

from Gladstone's Cabinet memorandum of May, 1882

L Gladstone reconsiders Anglo-Irish relations

About local government for Ireland, the ideas which more and more establish themselves in my mind are such as these.

1. Until we have seriously responsible bodies to deal with us in Ireland, every plan we frame comes to Irishmen, say what we may, as an English plan. As such it is probably condemned. At best it is a one-sided bargain, which binds us, not them. . .

4. In truth I should say, that for the Ireland of today, the first question is the rectification of the relations between landlord and tenant . . . the next is to relieve Great Britain from the enormous weight of the government of Ireland unaided by the people, and from the hopeless contradiction in which we stand while we give a parliamentary representation, hardly effective for anything but mischief without the local institutions of self-government which it presupposes, and on which alone it can have a sound and healthy basis.

Gladstone to W E Forster, April 1882

M Gladstone's reaction to the Phoenix Park murders

Uncle William . . . his face . . . like a prophet's in its look of faith and strength . . . came up and almost took me in his arms, and his first words were, 'Father, forgive them, for they know not what they do.' Then he said to me, 'Be assured it will not be in vain,' and across all my agony there fell a bright ray of hope, and I saw in a vision Ireland at peace, and my darling's life-blood accepted as a sacrifice for Christ's sake, to help to bring this to pass. . . I said to him as he was leaving me, 'Uncle William, you must never blame yourself for sending him.' He said, 'Oh no, there can be no question of that.'

from the journal of Lady Frederick Cavendish, May 1882

N Gladstone contemplates some form of home rule for Ireland

Under the present highly centralised system of Government, every demand, which can be started on behalf of a poor and ill-organised country, comes directly on the British Government and Treasury; if refused it becomes at once a head of grievance, if granted not only a new drain but a certain source of political complication and embarrassment, the peasant proprietary – the winter's distress – the state of the labourers – the loans to farmers – the promotion of public works – the encouragement of fisheries – the promotion of emigration – each and every one of these questions has a sting, and the sting can only be taken out of it by our treating it in correspondence with a popular and responsible Irish body – competent to act for its own portion of the country.

Gladstone to Granville, January 1883

O Gladstone's understanding of Home Rule
The conditions of an admissable plan are:

1. Union of the empire and due supremacy of parliament.

2. Protection for the minority – a difficult matter on which I have talked much with Spencer.

3. Fair allocation of imperial charges.

4. A statutory basis seems to me better and safer than the revival of Grattan's parliament.

5. Neither as opinions nor as intentions have I to any one alive promulgated these ideas as decided on by me.

6. As to intentions, I am determined to have none at present, to leave space to the government – I should wish to encourage them if I properly could – above all, on no account to say or do anything which would enable the nationalists to establish rival biddings between us.

Gladstone to Hartington, 17 December 1885

P Gladstone introduces the first Home Rule Bill, 1886
What are the results that have been produced [by the Act of union]? This result above all – and now I come to what I consider to be the basis of the whole mischief – that rightly or wrongly, yet in point of fact, law is discredited in Ireland, and discredited in Ireland upon this ground especially – that it comes to the people of that country with a foreign aspect, and in a foreign garb. . .

I ask you to show to Europe and to America that we, too can face political problems which America twenty years ago faced, and which many countries in Europe have been called upon to face, and have not feared to deal with. I ask that in our own case we should practise, with firm and fearless hand, what we have so often preached – that the concession of local self-government is not the way to sap or impair, but the way to strengthen and consolidate unity. I ask that we should apply to Ireland that happy experience which we gained in England and in Scotland . . . that the best and surest foundation we can find to build upon is the foundation afforded by the affections, the convictions, and the will of the nation; and it is thus, by the decree of the Almighty, that we may be enabled to secure at once the social peace, the fame, the power and the permanence of the Empire.

from Gladstone's speech in the Commons, April 1886

Q Gladstone's closing words on the Bill

Ireland stands at your bar expectant, hopeful, almost suppliant. Her words are the words of truth and soberness. She asks a blessed oblivion of the past, and in that oblivion our interest is deeper even than hers. You have been asked to-night to abide by the traditions of which we are the heirs. What traditions? By the Irish traditions? Go into the length and breadth of the world, ransack the literature of all countries, find if you can a single voice, a single book, in which the conduct of England towards Ireland is anywhere treated except with profound and bitter condemnation. Are these the traditions by which we are exhorted to stand? No, they are a sad exception to the glory of our country. They are a broad and black blot upon the pages of its history, and what we want to do is to stand by the traditions of which we are the heirs in all matters except our relations with Ireland, and to make our relation with Ireland to conform to the other traditions of our country. So we treat our traditions, so we hail the demand of Ireland for what I call a blessed oblivion of the past. She asks also a boon for the future; and that boon for the future, unless we are much mistaken, will be a boon to us in respect of honour, no less than a boon to her in respect of happiness, prosperity and peace. Such, sir, is her prayer. Think, I beseech you; think well, think wisely, think, not for the moment, but for the years that are to come, before you reject this Bill.

from Gladstone's speech on the second reading of the Home Rule Bill, 7 June 1886

R Gladstone on the impossibility of Parnell's continuing as leader of the Irish MPs

I thought it necessary, viewing the arrangements for the commencement of the session tomorrow, to acquaint Mr McCarthy with the conclusion at which, after using all the means of observation and reflection in my power, I had myself arrived. It was that notwithstanding the splendid services rendered by Mr Parnell to his country, his continuance at the present moment in the leadership would be productive of consequences disastrous in the highest degree to the cause of Ireland. I think I may be warranted in asking you so far to expand the conclusion I have given above, as to add that the continuance I speak of would not only place many hearty and effective friends of the Irish cause in a position of great embarrassment, but would render my retention of the leadership of the Liberal Party, based as it has been mainly upon the prosecution of the Irish cause, almost a nullity. This explanation of my views I begged Mr McCarthy to regard as confidential, and not intended for his colleagues generally, if he found that Mr Parnell contemplated spontaneous action; but I also begged that he would make known to the Irish party, at their meeting tomorrow afternoon, that such was my conclusion, if he should find that Mr Parnell had not in contemplation any step of the nature indicated. I now write to you, in case Mr McCarthy should be unable to communicate with Mr Parnell, as I understand you may possibly have an opening tomorrow through another channel. Should you have such an opening, I beg you to make known to Mr Parnell the conclusion itself, which I have stated in the earlier part of this letter.

Gladstone to John Morley, 24 November 1890

S Gladstone views the House of Lords as an obstacle to democracy
We are compelled to accompany that acceptance [of the Bill's defeat] with the sorrowful declaration that the differences, not of a temporary or causal nature merely, but differences of conviction, differences of fundamental tendency, between the House of Lords and the House of Commons, appear to have reached a development in the present year such as to create a state of things of which we are compelled to say that, in our judgment, it cannot continue. Sir, I do not wish to use hard words, which are easily employed and as easily retorted – it is a game that two can play at – but without using hard words, without presuming to judge of motives, without desiring or venturing to allege imputations, I have felt it a duty to state what appeared to me to be indisputable facts. The issue which is raised between a deliberative assembly, elected by the votes of more than 6,000,000 people, and a deliberative assembly occupied by many men of virtue, by many men of talent, of course with considerable diversities and varieties, is a controversy which, when once raised, must go forward to an issue.

from Gladstone's speech in the Commons, March 1894

Questions

1 Do Sources A–G indicate that Gladstone had accepted Disraeli's assessment of the Irish problem, as defined in Source A? **(7 marks)**

2 To what extent do Sources H, J, and O, illustrate Gladstone's earlier belief that the Irish question could be solved by the introduction of the necessary social and economic reforms? **(7 marks)**

3 In what ways do Sources I–M indicate the particular personal pressures which Gladstone was under in dealing with the Irish question? **(7 marks)**

4 Using your own knowledge and the evidence in Sources M–Q, comment on the view that Gladstone's move towards Home Rule was a logical progression. **(8 marks)**

5 Examine the significance of the following extracts:
  (a) '. . . his continuance at the present moment in the leadership would be productive of consequences disastrous in the highest degree to the cause of Ireland'. (Source R, line 6) **(7 marks)**
  (b) '. . . differences of fundamental tendency, between the House of Lords and the House of Commons'. (Source S, line 3) **(7 marks)**

8 DISRAELI AND THE EASTERN QUESTION

Disraeli's primary concern in foreign affairs was the protection of British interests. He never shared any of Gladstone's lofty concepts of internationalism and the concert of nations. His treatment of the Eastern Question is a vivid example of his basic attitude. In the nineteenth century Turkey was in a state of progressive collapse. For Britain, the Eastern Question was essentially a matter of safeguarding her national interests in the face of this. The fear was that as Turkey's hold over its Balkan and Middle Eastern territories weakened Russia would move in to assert her influence in those regions, thus threatening Britain's strategic and commerical position and the route to India [A–C].

Britain's entry into the Crimean War in the 1850s had been a demonstration of her anti-Russian suspicions. The Treaty of Paris that had ended that war had prohibited Russian war ships from entering the Black Sea. In 1871 Russia ignored that prohibition. Disraeli mocked Gladstone as Prime Minister for his failure to respond to this renewed Russian threat. Disraeli's anxieties about Russia were increased in the mid-1870s by the Turkish suppression of the Christians in Bulgaria. He feared that this might be used by Russia to justify an advance into the Balkans [D].

When in 1876 Gladstone published his impassioned anti-Turkish pamphlet *The Bulgarian Horrors and the Question of the East*, Disraeli attempted to counter it with ridicule [E–I]. He tried to answer Gladstone's constant charge that by supporting Turkey against Russia he was subordinating morality to expediency [J]. In 1877 Disraeli adopted an openly aggressive stance when he ordered British land and sea forces to the Dardenelles. This led to the resignation of his Foreign Secretary, Lord Derby [K].

It had been Disraeli's hope that he could persuade Germany and Austria to join Britain in imposing a settlement on Russia. This became more likely when Europe learned of the clauses of the Treaty of San Stefano which Russia forced upon Turkey in March 1878 [L–M]. Disraeli finally persuaded the major European nations to meet formally to reconsider the Eastern Question. Their gathering at the Congress of Berlin marked a major diplomatic success for Britain and an outstanding personal triumph for Disraeli. Bismarck, the German Chancellor, acknowledged the British Prime Minister as the dominant influence in shaping the Treaty of Berlin. Russia gave back most of the territories she had gained by San Stefano, 'Big Bulgaria' was subdivided, and Britain guaranteed to protect Turkey in return for the cession of Cyprus [N–Q].

A Disraeli's approach to foreign affairs

Disraeli added certain features peculiarly his own to the pattern with which he was to stamp the Conservative Party, and these enhanced the contrast with Gladstonian liberalism: belief in empire; adoption of a tough, 'no nonsense', foreign policy; assertion of Britain's, or as he would have said, England's, greatness in the world. Disraeli was unsympathetic to all forms of nationalism except English nationalism . . . and he saw no reason, whether in Ireland or the Balkans or elsewhere, to allow what he considered English interests to be overridden by the supposedly higher moral law that encourages the emancipation of nations 'rightly struggling to be free'.

from *Disraeli* by Robert Blake (1966)

B Disraeli defines England's role

Since the settlement [of 1815] . . . England . . . has on the whole followed a Conservative foreign policy. I do not mean by a Conservative foreign policy a foreign policy that would disapprove – still less oppose – the natural development of nations, I mean a foreign policy interested in the tranquility and prosperity of the world, the normal condition of which is peace, and which does not ally itself with the revolutionary party of Europe. Other countries have their political systems and public objects, as England had, though they may not have attained them. She is not to look upon them with unreasonable jealousy. The position of England in the Councils of Europe is essentially that of a moderating and mediatorial Power. Her interest and her policy are, when changes are inevitable and necessary, to assist so that these changes, if possible, may be accomplished without war, or if war occurs, that its duration and asperity may be lessened. That is what I mean by the just influence of England in the Councils of Europe. . .

from a speech by Disraeli, 1864

C Disraeli's view of the Eastern Question

The Eastern Question, as it presented itself to Disraeli in the seventies, was one side of the great problem how to safeguard the British Empire, with its immense commercial and territorial interests in the Levant, in the Persian Gulf, in India, in Australasia, and in the Far East, in face of a simultaneous and sweeping advance of Russian power and propaganda, both in Europe and in Asia, towards the south and the sea.

from *Life of Disraeli* by G E Buckle (1920)

D Disraeli is determined to oppose Russian expansion
Lord Beaconsfield has great hopes of being able to settle this great
question, but of course guarded himself against any opinion as to
Peace or War. Supposing the Russians do enter Bulgaria, said I. That,
he answered, would be an entirely new phase of the question. He is
evidently quite determined that the Russians shall not directly, or
indirectly, become possessed of Constantinople.

Many in England say, Why not? England might take Egypt, and so
secure our highway to India.

But the answer is obvious, said Lord B. If the Russians had
Constantinople, they could at any time march their Army through
Syria to the mouth of the Nile, and then what would be the use of
our holding Egypt? Not even the command of the sea could help us
under such circumstances. People who talk in this manner must be
utterly ignorant of geography. Our strength is on the sea.
Constantinople is the key of India, and not Egypt and the Suez Canal.

The mendacity of the Russians is the same as ever. They say: 'We
do not wish to hold Constantinople.' Perhaps not, but for all that their
game is to have someone there who is more or less dependent on
them.

from a memorandum by Lord Barrington, October 1876

**E Initially, Disraeli chose to regard the reports of the Bulgarian
atrocities as exaggerations**
I cannot doubt that atrocities have been committed in Bulgaria; but
that girls were sold into slavery, or that more than 10,000 persons
have been imprisoned, I doubt. In fact, I doubt whether there is prison
accommodation for so many, or that torture has been practised on a
great scale among an Oriental people who seldom, I believe, resort
to torture, but generally terminate their connection with culprits in a
more expeditious manner.

from a speech in the Commons by Disraeli, 10 July 1876

F
A consul hears, and no doubt truly, that there has been some
extremely wild work on the part of some of the Bashi-Bazouks, and
he engages someone to go to a coffee house frequented by these
ruffians, where he listens to the reports of the wild work that has
been going on. One present says '5000 or 6000 must have perished
innocently', when another answers 'if you had said 25,000 or 26,000
you would have been more correct', as if exulting in the carnage. . . I
was not justified for a moment to adopt that coffee house babble
brought by an anonymous Bulgarian to a consul as at all furnishing

a basis of belief that the accounts subsequently received had any justification.

from a speech in the Commons by Disraeli, 31 July 1876

G However, the reports from Bulgaria became increasingly graphic and disturbing.
After stating that the insurrection was repressed, Mr Baring [*The Times* correspondent] proceeds to show how this was done. He first enumerates the charges published in England – that cartloads of heads had been paraded about the streets of different towns; that women and children had been publicly sold in the streets . . . that horrible tortures had been practised on the prisoners . . . that at least 25,000 perfectly innocent persons had been massacred; and that a large number of villages, differently stated as between 60 and 100, had been burnt.

from *The Times*, 20 September 1876

H Disraeli's verdict on Gladstone's pamphlet
Gladstone has had the impudence to send me his pamphlet, tho' he accuses me of several crimes. The document is passionate and not strong; vindictive and ill-written – that of course. Indeed, in that respect, of all the Bulgarian horrors, perhaps the greatest.

Disraeli to Lord Derby, September 1876

I Disraeli mocks Gladstone's solemnity
Designing politicians might take advantage of such sublime sentiments [as expressed by Gladstone], and apply them for the furtherance of their sinister ends.

   I am quite convinced that Mr Gladstone on reflection never intended anything of the kind. If he had gone to the House of Commons and had proposed to the House of Commons and the Speaker to attend Greenwich Fair, and go to the top of Greenwich Hill and all roll down to the bottom, I declare he could not have proposed anything more absurdly incongruous.

from Disraeli's speech at Aylesbury, September 1876

J Disraeli argues that to defend Turkey is to protect English interests
We are, it is true, the allies of the Sultan of Turkey. . . . We guarantee with France and Austria the territorial integrity of Turkey. These are our engagements, and they are the engagements that we endeavour to fulfil. And if these engagements, renovated and repeated only four years ago by the wisdom of Europe, are to be treated . . . as idle wind

and chaff, and if we are to be told that our political duty is by force to expel the Turks to the other side of the Bosphorus, then politics cease to be an art, statesmanship becomes a mere mockery.

I am sure that as long as England is ruled by English Parties who understand the principles on which our Empire is founded, and who are resolved to maintain that Empire, our influence in that part of the world can never be looked upon with indifference. . . Those who suppose that England ever would uphold, or at this moment particularly is upholding, Turkey from blind superstition, and from a want of sympathy with the highest aspirations of humanity, are deceived. What our duty is at this critical moment is to maintain the Empire of England. Nor will we ever agree to any step, though it may obtain for a moment comparative quiet and a false prosperity, that hazards the existence of that Empire.

from a speech by Disraeli in the Commons, 1876

K Disraeli's Foreign Secretary resigns

I know our chief of old, and from various things that have dropped from him I am fully convinced — not indeed that he wants war — but that he has made up his mind to large military preparations, to an extremely warlike speech, to an agitation in favour of armed intervention (recollect that he said in Cabinet: 'The country is asleep and I want to wake it up'), and if possible to an expedition that shall occupy Constantinople or Gallipoli. . .

His views are different from mine where such matters are concerned, not in detail but in principle. He believes thoroughly in 'prestige' as all foreigners do, and would think it (quite sincerely) in the interests of the country to spend 200 millions on a war if the result was to make foreign States think more highly of us as a military power. These ideas are intelligible, but they are not mine nor yours and their being sincerely held does not make them less dangerous.

Derby to Salisbury, December 1877

L Salisbury, Disraeli's new Foreign Secretary, condemns the San Stefano Treaty of 1878

By the articles erecting the new Bulgaria, a strong Slav state will be created under the auspices and control of Russia, possessing important harbours upon the shores of the Black Sea and the Archipelago, and conferring upon that Power a preponderating influence upon both political and commercial relations in those seas. . .

The provisions by which this new state is to be subjected to a ruler whom Russia will practically choose, its administration framed by a

Russian Commissary, and the first working of its institutions
commenced under the control of the Russian Army, sufficiently
indicate the political system of which in future it is to form a part. . .
These various stipulations . . . depress, almost to the point of entire
subjection, the political independence of the Government of
Constantinople . . . Of the deepest interest to Great Britain . . . is the
power of the Ottoman Government to close or to open the Straits.

from a report by Salisbury, March 1878

M Disraeli's description of the Treaty

The Treaty of San Stefano completely abrogates what is known as
Turkey-in-Europe; it abolishes the dominion of the Ottoman Empire
in Europe; it creates a large State which, under the name of Bulgaria,
is inhabited by many races not Bulgarians. This Bulgaria goes to the
shores of the Black Sea and seizes the ports of that coast. The treaty
provides for the government of this new Bulgaria, under a prince
who is to be selected by Russia; its administration is to be organised
and supervised by a commissary of Russia; and this new State is to
be garrisoned, I say for an indefinite period, but at all events for two
years certain, by Russia.

from a speech by Disraeli in the Lords, April 1878

N Disraeli's triumphant return from Berlin in 1878

Our representatives at the Congress, the EARL OF BEACONSFIELD
and the MARQUIS OF SALISBURY met with an enthusiastic reception
on their arrival in London, and the Order of the Garter were confirmed
on both these statesmen almost immediately by Her Majesty.

The existence of the Convention between England and Turkey . . .
was known in June, but its provisions were not published until 8
July, a few days before the close of the Congress. The principal article
was to the following effect:

'. . . if any attempt shall be made at any future time by Russia to
take possession of any further territories of his Imperial Majesty the
SULTAN in Asia, as fixed by the definitive Treaty of Peace, England
engages to join the SULTAN in defending them by force of arms. In
return the SULTAN promises to England to introduce necessary
reforms to be agreed upon later between the two Powers, into the
Government; and, for the protection of the Christian and other
subjects of the Porte in these territories, and in order to enable
England to make necessary provision for executing her engagements,
the SULTAN further consents to assign the Island of Cyprus, to be
occupied and administered by England.'

from *Punch*, July 1878

O **Crowds at Charing Cross on Disraeli's return from Berlin in 1878**

P Disraeli claims to have achieved 'peace with honour'
In Dover and in London the return of Lord Beaconsfield and Lord
Salisbury won a popular ovation. The London, Chatham and Dover
twin steamer the *Calais-Douvres*, in which Lord Beaconsfield and Lord
Salisbury travelled, put alongside the Admiralty Pier at 2.40. There
was a large crowd which cheered heartily, and a local band struck up
'Home, Sweet Home'. The town and the shipping in Dover harbour
were decorated. . . The following address, which was very beautifully
illuminated, was presented to Lord Beaconsfield. . . 'May it please your
Lordship – We, the members of the Dover Workingmen's
Constitutional Association, humbly bid your Lordship a cordial
welcome to our shores on your return from that Congress at whose
deliberations, by the blessing of God, you have, by your great intellect
and firm demeanour, added so materially to the restoration of the
peace of Empires and the assertion of England's might and position
among nations. . .'
   Lord Beaconsfield, in reply, said – 'I do not like to go away without
thanking you for the very kind manner in which you have received
me and my colleague Lord Salisbury. We have brought a peace, and
we trust we have brought a peace with honour'.

from *The Times*, 17 July 1878

Q A modern verdict on Disraeli's achievement

Judged by the criteria of tactical skill and achievement of objectives, Disraeli's foreign policy was an undoubted success. As for the Berlin settlement, of course it was not perfect. No treaty ever is. But it was followed by almost as long a period of peace between the European great powers as the interval separating the Crimean War from the Congress of Vienna. As one of the two principal plenipotentiaries at Berlin Disraeli must share with Bismarck some part of the credit.

from *Disraeli* by Robert Blake (1966)

Questions

1 To what extent do Sources A, B, C and D concur in their presentation of Disraeli's attitude towards foreign affairs and the Eastern Question?
(8 marks)

2 How far does the evidence in Sources E–I substantiate the view that Disraeli's response to the Bulgarian atrocities was determined not by the merits of the case but by his personal rivalry with Gladstone?
(8 marks)

3 Does the attitude expressed in Source J justify Derby's assertion in Source K that in foreign affairs Disraeli was concerned solely with maintaining national prestige? **(8 marks)**

4 Using your own knowledge and the evidence in Sources N, P and Q, judge how effectively the Treaty of Berlin had reversed the effects of the Treaty of San Stefano, as described in Sources L and M.
(9 marks)

9 GLADSTONE AND THE EASTERN QUESTION

In 1874 Gladstone withdrew from politics with the declared intention of studying theology and preparing himself for death. Two years later the Turkish atrocities in Bulgaria brought him thundering out of retirement. So began what historians call his second political career, which was to last another twenty years.

In the 1870s the Eastern Question became for the British one of those great moral issues that divided the nation. The personal antipathy between Gladstone and Beaconsfield (Disraeli) reached its deepest over the Eastern Question.

A Richard Shannon, the major modern authority on the subject, emphasises that Gladstone's remarkable contribution to the debate was not to create the national mood but to respond to it.
The 'Bulgarian atrocities agitation' was the greatest public incursion into the official conduct of foreign affairs in British history. Hundreds of meetings denounced the government's pro-Turkish policy and demanded that it be reversed in the direction of Christian and national emancipation. By 22 August [1876], Derby warned . . . that the 'universal feeling of indignation' had reached such a pitch that in the extreme case of Russia declaring war on the Turks the British government would find it 'practically impossible to interfere'. The Bulgarian issue was a seismic shock which opened the national faultlines. The Conservative Party was affected least of all. Apart from a few renegade High Churchmen there was no move of revolt or dissent. The Liberal Party was much more vulnerable to the tremors. By and large the party went with the agitation, though the movement always remained essentially an 'out of doors' phenomenon, leading the politicians rather than being led by them.

The agitation was undoubtedly the vehicle of a great deal of politics, secular and religious. Joseph Chamberlain, the emerging leader of the Radicals, cared little for the Bulgarians but a great deal for the chances of Gladstone's return to the leadership at the expense of the Whigs. But beyond this level of concern lay the true significance of the agitation. It manifested on the largest scale a public conscience stricken with a sense of complicity in political transactions of the utmost immorality. . .

Gladstone's eventual intervention of 6 September 1876 – the famous pamphlet *Bulgarian Horrors and the Question of the East* – was one of the most dramatic acts of his enormous career. Overnight it made him the leader and public spokesman of the agitation against Disraeli's eastern policy. Belatedly he had come to realise that the 'masses', so inert in 1874, had recovered their moral sense. As he put it: 'the game was afoot and the question yet alive'.

from *The Crisis of Imperialism, 1865–1914* by Richard Shannon (1974)

B Gladstone's pamphlet

We now know in detail that there have been perpetrated . . . crimes and outrages so vast in scale as to exceed all modern example, and so utterly vile as well as fierce in character, that it passes the power of heart to conceive, and of tongue and pen adequately to describe them. These are the Bulgarian horrors . . . the elaborate and refined cruelty – the only refinement of which Turkey boasts! – the utter disregard of sex and age – the abominable and beastly lust, and the entire and violent lawlessness which still stalks over the land . . . murdering, burning, impaling, roasting men and women and children indiscriminately, with the extremist refinements of cruelty. . .

The matter has become too painfully real for us to be scared by the hobgoblin of Russia. . . It is now too late to argue . . . that it might be quite proper that twelve or thirteen millions of Christians in Turkey should remain unhappy, rather than that . . . two hundred millions of men in India should be deprived of the benefits of British rule. . .

An old servant of the Crown and State, I entreat my countrymen . . . that our Government, which has been working in one direction, shall work in the other; and shall apply all its vigour to concur with the other States of Europe in obtaining the extinction of the Turkish executive power in Bulgaria. Let the Turks now carry away their abuses in the only possible manner, namely by carrying off themselves. Their Zaptiehs and their Mudirs, their Bimbashis and their Yuzbachis, their Kaimakams and their Pashas, one all, bag and baggage, shall, I hope, clear out from the provinces they have desolated and profaned. This thorough riddance, this most blessed deliverance, is the only reparation that we can make to the memory of those heaps on heaps of dead, to the violated purity alike of matron, of maiden and of child; to the civilisation which has been affronted and shamed, to the laws of God or, if you like, Allah; to the moral sense of mankind at large. There is not a criminal in a European gaol, there is not a cannibal in the South Sea Islands, whose indignation would not rise and overboil at the recital of that which has been done, which has too late been examined, but which remains unavenged.

from *'The Bulgarian Horrors and the Question of the East'* by W E Gladstone (1876)

C Gladstone invading Egypt

D Gladstone backs the 'masses' against the 'classes'

There is an undoubted and smart rally on behalf of Turkey in the
metropolitan press. It is in the main representative of the ideas and
opinions of what are called the upper ten thousand. From this body
there has never on any occasion within my memory proceeded the
impulse that has prompted, and finally achieved, *any* of the great
measures which in the last half century have contributed so much to
the fame and happiness of England. They did not emancipate the
dissenters, Roman Catholics, and Jews. They did not reform the
parliament. They did not liberate the negro slave. They did not abolish
the corn law. They did not take the taxes off the press. They did not
abolish the Irish established church. They did not cheer on the work of
Italian freedom and reconstitution. Yet all these things have been
done; and done by other agencies than theirs, and despite their
opposition. When I speak of *them*, I speak of course of the majority
among them. Unhappily, the country is understood abroad mainly
through the metroplitan press.

Gladstone to Madame Novikov, October 1876

E Gladstone suggests that it is Disraeli's Jewishness that makes him pro-Turkish and anti-Christian
I have a strong suspicion that Dizzy's crypto-Judaism has had to do with his policy. The Jews of the east hate the Christians; who have not always used them well.

Gladstone to the Duke of Argyll, 1876

F
Disraeli may be willing to risk his government for his Judaic feeling – the deepest and truest . . . in his whole mind.

Gladstone to his wife, 1876

G Disraeli doubts Gladstone's sanity
Posterity will do justice to that unprincipled maniac Gladstone – extraordinary mixture of envy, vindictiveness, hypocrisy, and superstition; and with one commanding characteristic – whether Prime Minister, or Leader of the Opposition, whether preaching, praying, speechifying, or scribbling – never a gentleman.

Disraeli to Lady Bradford, 1876

H Gladstone presses the moral argument in Parliament, claiming that, but for Disraeli's leadership, the members of the Government would follow their conscience and abandon the pro-Turkish policy.
There were other days when England was the hope of freedom. Wherever in the world a high aspiration was entertained, or a noble blow was struck, it was to England that the eyes of the oppressed were always turned – to this favourite, this darling home of so much privilege and so much happiness, where the people that had built up a noble edifice for themselves would, it was well known, be ready to do what in them lay to secure the benefit of the same inestimable boon for others. There is now before the world a glorious prize. A portion of those unhappy people are still as yet making an effort to retrieve what they have lost so long, but have not ceased to love and desire. I speak of those in Bosnia and Herzegovina. Another portion – a band of heroes such as the world has rarely seen – stand on the rocks of Montenegro, and are ready now, as they have ever been during the 400 years of their exile from their fertile plains, to sweep down from the fastnesses and meet the Turks at any odds for the re-establishment of justice and of peace in those countries. Another portion still, the 5,000,000 of Bulgarians, cowed and beaten down to the ground, hardly venturing to look upwards, even to their Father in heaven, have extended their hands to you; they have sent you their petition, they have prayed for your help and protection. They have

told you that they do not seek alliance with Russia, or with any foreign power, but that they seek to be delivered from an intolerable burden of woe and shame. That burden of woe and shame – the greatest that exists on God's earth – is one that we thought united Europe was about to remove; but to removing which, for the present, you seem to have no efficacious means of offering even the smallest practical contribution. But, sir, the removal of that load of woe and shame is a great and noble prize. It is a prize well worth competing for. It is not yet too late to try to win it. I believe there are men in the cabinet who would try to win it, if they were free to act on their own beliefs and aspirations. It is not yet too late, I say, to become competitors for that prize; but be assured that whether you mean to claim for yourselves even a single leaf in that immortal chaplet of renown, which will be the reward of true labour in that cause, or whether you turn your backs upon that cause and upon your own duty, I believe, for one, that the knell of Turkish tyranny in these provinces has sounded. So far as human eye can judge, it is about to be destroyed. The destruction may not come in the way or by the means that we should choose; but come this boon from what hands it may, it will be a noble boon, and as a noble boon will gladly be accepted by Christendom and the world.

from a speech by Gladstone in the Commons, May 1877

I On occasion, Gladstone faced violent demonstrations, which he did not regard as spontaneous
Feb 24 [18]78 – Between four and six, three parties of the populace arrived here, the first with cheers, the two others hostile. Windows were broken and much hooting. The last detachment was only kept away by mounted police in line across the street both ways. This is not very sabbatical. There is strange work behind the curtain, if one could only get at it. The instigators are those really guilty; no one can wonder at the tools.

from the *Gladstone Diaries* (*op cit*)

J Gladstone refused to share in the general rejoicing that followed Disraeli's apparent triumph at the Congress of Berlin in 1878. He considered that Britain had been unworthily represented
I say, sir, that in this congress of the great Powers, the voice of England has not been heard in unison with the institutions, the history, and the character of England. . . I do not mean that [Lord Beaconsfield and Lord Salisbury] ought to have gone to the congress determined to insist upon the unqualified prevalence of what I may call British ideas. They were bound to act in consonance with the

general views of Europe. But . . . I do affirm that it was their part to take the side of liberty; and I do also affirm that as a matter of fact they took the side of servitude. . .

I think we have lost greatly by the conclusion of this convention; I think we have lost very greatly indeed the sympathy and respect of the nations of Europe. I do not expect or believe that we shall fall into that sort of contempt which follows upon weakness. I think it to be one of the most threadbare of all the weapons of the party warfare when we hear, as we sometimes hear, on the accession of a new government, that before its accession the government of England had been despised all over the world, and that now on the contrary she has risen in the general estimation, and holds her proper place in the councils of nations. This England of ours is not so poor and so weak a thing as to depend upon the reputation of this or that administration; and the world knows pretty well of what stuff she is made.

. . . The proceedings have all along been associated with a profession as to certain British interests, which although I believe them to be perfectly fictitious and imaginary, have yet been pursued with as much zeal and eagerness as if they had been the most vital realities in the world. This setting up of our own interests, out of place, in an exaggerated form, beyond their proper sphere, and not merely the setting up of such interests, but the mode in which they have been pursued, has greatly diminished, not, as I have said, the regard for our material strength, but the estimation of our moral standard of action, and consequently our moral position in the world.

from Gladstone's speech in the Commons, July 1978

K Stung by Gladstone's description of the Treaty of Berlin as 'an insane convention', Disraeli replied spiritedly
But I would put this issue to an English jury. Which do you believe most likely to enter an insane convention, a body of English gentlemen honoured by the favour of their Sovereign and the confidence of their fellow-subjects, managing your affairs for five years, I hope with prudence, and not altogether without success, or a sophistical rhetorician, inebriated with the exuberance of his own verbosity, and gifted with an egotistical imagination that can at all times command an interminable and inconsistent series of arguments to malign an opponent and to glorify himself?

from Disraeli's speech at Knightsbridge, July 1878

L How personalised the Eastern Question had become for the two protagonists was indicated by a letter of Disraeli's to Gladstone at this time

Lord Beaconsfield presents his compliments to Mr Gladstone, and has the honour to acknowledge the receipt of his letter of this day's date, referring to some remarks made by Lord Beaconsfield last night in the House of Lords, and requesting to be supplied with a list of epithets applied, not merely to Lord Beaconsfield's measures, but to his person and character, and with a note of the times and places at which they were used.

As this would involve a research over a period of two years and a half, Lord Beaconsfield, who is at this moment much pressed with affairs, is obliged to request those gentlemen, who are kind enough to assist him in the conduct of public business, to undertake the necessary researches, which probably may require some little time; but that Lord Beaconsfield, by such delay in replying to Mr Gladstone, may not appear wanting in becoming courtesy, he must observe with reference to the Oxford speech referred to in the House of Lords, and which was one long invective against the government, that Mr Gladstone then remarked that, when he spoke of the Government, he meant Lord Beaconsfield, who was alone responsible, and by whom 'the great name of England had been degraded and debased.'

In the same spirit a few days back at Southwark, Lord Beaconsfield was charged with 'an act of duplicity of which every Englishman should be ashamed, an act of duplicity which has not been surpassed, and, Mr Gladstone believed, 'has been rarely equalled in the history of nations.' Such an act, however, might be expected from a Minister who, according to Mr Gladstone, had 'sold the Greeks'.

With regard to the epithet 'devilish' which Lord Beaconsfield used in the House of Lords, he is informed that it was not Mr Gladstone at Hawarden who compared Lord Beaconsfield to Mephistopheles, but only one of Mr Gladstone's friends, kindly enquiring of Mr Gladstone how they were 'to get rid of this Mephistopheles': but as Mr Gladstone proceeded to explain the mode, probably the Birmingham caucus, Lord Beaconsfield may perhaps be excused for assuming that Mr Gladstone sanctioned the propriety of the scarcely complimentary appellation.

Disraeli to Gladstone, 30 July 1878

M A modern assessment of Gladstone and the Eastern Question

The Eastern Question, reinforced by the subsequent difficulties of the Tory Government in Southern Africa and on the Indian frontier, thus brought Gladstone to a bold and prophetic analysis of Britain's possible position in the future world order. He freely and without regret accepted the natural relative decline of Britain's industrial supremacy, and the ending of her unique position, especially through the growth of the USA. Since Britain's power rested on the strength of her domestic economy, and since that power would in the long run be relatively declining, imperial expansion, justifiable though it might be in particular instances, must be resisted. Otherwise a position would be reached where a relatively declining power sought vainly to defend and control a vast Empire whose new acquisitions would each multiply the points of danger, conflict, and potential crisis. An anxious Edwardian could hardly have put it better.

Gladstone thus held that an independently British policy towards the Straits, separate from the Concert's concern at civilised standards of behaviour in Turkey, was unnecessary, undesirable, and dangerous. There was no unique 'British interest', and there should therefore be no unilateral British action. Indeed, the assertion of a British interest independent of that of Europe played into the hands of Russia, for it left Britain the prisoner of the Turks, while allowing the Russians to appear as the sole champions of Christians in the Balkans, a role which they had, in Gladstone's view, been permitted by the Treaty of Kuchuk Kainardji (1774), but which they had ceded to the Concert at the end of the Crimean War in 1856. To have allowed the Russians to reclaim, by default, their pre–1854 position, was a further danger. The Conservative Cabinet's policy in 1876 had allowed Russia to 'associate all Europe with her', with the danger of a Russo-Turkish agreement, settling 'matters in such a way as to leave all Europe out of account'.

from the Introduction to *The Gladstone Diaries* (vol ix) by H C G Matthew (1986)

Questions

1 How important to the historian are Sources B and D as evidence of Gladstone's backing of the 'masses' against the 'classes'? **(8 marks)**

2 To what extent does the evidence in Sources E, F, G, I and L suggest that the dispute betwen Disraeli and Gladstone over Turkey was more a matter of personality than of principle? **(8 marks)**

3 In what ways is Source H illustrative of Gladstone's attempt to lift the argument over the Eastern Question from the political to the moral sphere? **(7 marks)**

4 According to the evidence in Sources J and K what were Gladstone's main objections to the Conservative Government's policy towards Turkey? **(7 marks)**

5 How far do the analyses of the modern scholars, as expressed in Sources A and M, suggest that Gladstone's stand on the Eastern Question was part of his broader design to bring a greater sense of reality to British foreign policy? **(10 marks)**

10 GLADSTONE AND DISRAELI – THE HISTORICAL PERSPECTIVE

Gladstone and Disraeli were controversial figures in their own time. Although modern historians are much more in agreement in their estimates of the two statesmen, individual scholars tend to emphasise different aspects of their significance.

A Philip Magnus, the first biographer to make extensive use of Gladstone's 'Diaries', identifies the three outstanding phases of Gladstone's career

In the first phase, when he was Chancellor of the Exchequer, Gladstone achieved unparalleled success in his policy of setting the individual free from a multitude of obsolete restrictions. He thereby implemented his creed that self-discipline in freedom is the essential condition of the mental health of men and nations, as well as of their material prosperity. The crowning moments were the great Budgets of 1853 and 1860. Gladstone's reputation was made in the field of finance, to which, under Sir Robert Peel's guidance, he graduated directly from that of theology.

During the second phase of his career, Gladstone achieved great success in arousing the moral indignation of the British people against Turkish misrule in the Balkans, and against what he regarded as Disraeli's blindness – typifying that of the great and cautious world – to the transcendental issues which are involved in all tryanny and oppression. The crowning moment was the Midlothian campaign of 1879. Gladstone's efforts in that cause made him the foremost statesman in Great Britain and a moral force in Europe.

During the third and final phase of his career, Gladstone, in his magnificent old age, led a crusade against English misrule in Ireland. The crowning moments were the rejections of his first and second Home Rule Bills in 1886 and 1893. The lamentable results of those two resounding failures belong to history; they were due in part to temperamental defects in Gladstone himself, in part to accident, but mainly to the fact that Gladstone's principal opponents and colleagues were more worldly, and ultimately less far-sighted and high-minded, than he was. Gladstone was undaunted in the face of humiliation and defeat. He towered in moral grandeur over his contemporaries and stood before the world as the inspired prophet of the nineteenth-century liberal experiment.

from *Gladstone* by Philip Magnus (1954)

B Agatha Ramm, a renowned analyst of British political history, looks at the basis of the legendary animosity between Gladstone and Disraeli

The rivalry between them, or rather their mutual hostility, was ineradicable after Gladstone followed Disraeli as Chancellor of the Exchequer, succeeded with *his* budget whereas Disraeli had failed in his. Gladstone's second budget and the slip Disraeli made in opposing its provision for an increase in the malt tax was the cause of Gladstone's ascendancy. . .

[Gladstone's] transition to popular politics was made during the administrations of 1859 to 1866 by reaching a conclusion in a complex train of thought which related finance and the franchise. Gladstone lowered the level at which income tax became payable from £150 to £100 annual income. He believed he was bringing into the payers of income tax a kind of responsible citizen, who might also have the vote, for he would have interest in keeping down expenditure.

One can further discern three distinctive features of Gladstone's practice that established his new position with the electorate. In the 1860s Gladstone became known outside the Court, Westminster and Oxford: in Wales and in Scotland where he was Rector of Edinburgh University from 1860–5. He became, in short, a national figure by speeches at political meetings subsequently reported in columns of close print in *The Times* and other papers. In 1862 in the towns of Tyneside and Lancashire he made a series of backward-looking speeches on his achievements. He received trade union deputations and made contact in London with the trade union junta. He continued throughout the 1860s to speak to large audiences of middle- and working-class men and women in provincial towns.

Secondly he made astute use of the growth of the newspaper press. By the Crimean War period the telegram brought news to the newspapers speedily; steam presses speeded up their printing, and the railway their distribution. His abolition of the paper duties in 1861 was the prelude to a rapid expansion of the provincial and the metropolitan press. Gladstone used the *Daily Telegraph*. Owned by the Levi-Lawson family, and at the price of 1d and a circulation of 200,000, it outdistanced *The Times* whose monopoloy of upper-class readers it ended. It quickly absorbed the Peelite *Morning Chronicle* and profited from the advantages which Gladstone put in the way of its reporters. In return, it was the *Daily Telegraph* which created the image of the People's William.

Thirdly Gladstone combined an exact attention to publicity with a most advantageous appearance of unworldliness. He supplied the press with a constant flow of information about his movements and intentions when out of office in 1855–9, and timely releases when in office. There were no untimely or premature leaks of information until the 1880s. He had 'constructed for himself a constituency in the country'. From the autumn session of 1867 Gladstone was already master of the situation and carrying measures through the Commons against the Derby-Disraeli government which was still in office.

from *Gladstone as Politician* by Agatha Ramm (1980)

C H C G Matthew, the editor of *The Gladstone Diaries*, analyses Gladstone's key role in changing British social and political attitudes

'Men make their own history, but none of their own free will; not under circumstances they themselves have chosen but under the given and inherited circumstances with which they are directly confronted.' Of few can Marx's truism be truer than of William Ewart Gladstone. His epic public career – first in office in 1834, last in 1894 – confronted the prime of Britain as the first industrial nation. The agenda of free trade and imperialism was dictated by forces far beyond the control of individuals acting as such. Yet the interpretation and execution of the agenda was achieved by the decisions and actions of individuals . . . In the process through which the British governing class came to terms with its new commercial and industrial destiny, Gladstone was a vital agent.

Forged by an education essentially pre-industrial, Gladstone mirrored his times in adapting politically, religiously, and socially to new circumstances. A radical conservatism, which fused at times with an advanced Liberalism, was Gladstone's method. It was a method which deeply perplexed Conservatives, and often disappointed Liberals. For the former, it was almost always too much, too soon; for the latter, it was sometimes too little, too late. But it came to give Gladstone a curious position of great power in the centre of British politics, the power of surprise, of resource, of stability, and of an appeal, after the 1830s, that history and time were on his side.

In all this, the fixed point for Gladstone was his Christian faith, the preservation of the Church and the triumph of Christian values.

As a chief representative of the Victorian age, Gladstone's career displays the strengths and weaknesses of a liberal democracy at the height of its self-confidence. The powerful individualism, the executive competence, the capacity for a sense of history, a feel for 'ripeness' and for national develoment; against these may be balanced, for all the introspection, a curious lack of self-awareness.

from *Gladstone 1809–74* by H C G Matthew (1986)

D Richard Shannon, the writer of a large-scale biography of Gladstone, based on the published *Diaries*, contrasts the attitude of Disraeli and Gladstone towards change and reform

Unlike Disraeli . . . Gladstone was excited by large ideas of imaginative creativity. The fact that circumstances made him play but a sorry role in the actual matter of the reform issue in 1866 and 1867 did nothing to dampen this excitement. Rather, his indignation made him all the more determined to scotch Disraeli, and eventually earned him the awed tribute that he was 'terrible on the rebound'. But his pilgrimage towards 'light and freedom' requires to be examined with care and reservations. Gladstone used language in a manner peculiar to his time which requires to be decoded to avoid confusion. When Gladstone used words like 'future', 'time is on our side', 'great social forces', 'firm hands of a united people', 'certain and not distant victory', they have no necessary objective validity. In fact in practically every respect Gladstone's assumptions about the shape of the future were belied by events, just as were Disraeli's assumptions about the possibilities of perpetuating a traditional Palmerstonian past. In what amounts to a contest in misapprehension between these two great national leaders in the coming decades Gladstone, as it happens, came off rather the worse through no great fault of his own and no great merit in Disraeli. But for purposes of immediate analysis it must be stressed that the day-to-day range of Gladstone's imagination did not reach significantly beyond the boundaries of Liberalism as variously defined by Mill, Bright and others. He would never go with Mill in the direction of socialistic 'constructionism'; he would never go with Bright against the Church and into a diplomacy of isolationism . . .

Near the end of his life, Gladstone looked back over his career and tried to analyse what it was about his approach to politics that most distinguished him. His analysis, in a memorandum of about 1896, is worthy of careful attention because of its extraordinary penetration in a general way and because of its particular value as evidence on specific points of later controversies. If, he wrote, providence had endowed him with anything that could be called a 'striking gift' it was that he had the power of divining at 'certain political junctures' 'what may be termed appreciation of the general situation and its result.' By this Gladstone was careful to insist that he did not mean a mere opportunism, 'a simple acceptance of public opinion, founded upon the discernment that it has risen to a certain height needful for a given work, like a tide'. On the contrary, it was something much more positive, exalted and creative: 'It is an insight into the facts of particular eras, and their relations one to another, which generates in the mind a conviction that the materials exist for forming a public opinion, and for directing it to a particular end'. Gladstone considered that there were four such crucial occasions in his career: the renewal of the income tax in 1853; the 'proposal of religious equality for Ireland' in 1868; Home Rule for Ireland in 1886; and his attempt to get his last cabinet to agree in 1894 to a confrontation with the House of Lords.

from *The Crisis of Imperialism, 1865–1915* by Richard Shannon (1974)

E Lord Blake, the author of the definitive modern biography of Disraeli, compares the characters of Gladstone and Disraeli and assesses their place in British political history

At times one feels that Disraeli's antipathy to Gladstone – and Gladstone's to Disraeli – was not simply caused by the differences of their political outlook on concrete issues, important though these were, but rather by their whole approach to politics, their way of thinking, their political style. What Disraeli disliked was the bringing of morality and religion into politics – to him an essentially practical business. By the same token Gladstone deplored the cynical amorality of his old enemy. . .

One could probably say of them as parliamentarians that honours were even. As ministers, no. The most ardent admirer of Disraeli must concede that Gladstone was more thorough, more knowledgeable, more energetic, better briefed. One has only to contrast the slapdash nature of Disraeli's first budget (1852), in which he muddled up all the income tax schedules, with the immensely competent and carefully planned first budget of Gladstone the following year. And Gladstone, who was of course in office far more than Disraeli, showed his superiority in the field of legislation again and again. The contrast in the length of their official experience is worth mentioning. Down to Disraeli's death in April 1881, Gladstone had been in office for nineteen and a half years, Disraeli only eleven. More strikingly perhaps, Gladstone had had thirteen years of official experience before he became Prime Minister, Disraeli less than four – figures which of course reflect the fact that for half a century or more after 1832 the Liberals were the normal majority party. In common they had their apprenticeship at the Exchequer. Disraeli held no other post before he reached the top. Gladstone held it for nine years all told. It is partly because of them that the Chancellorship became so important. Hitherto the second man in the government had usually been at the Foreign or Home Office. The Foreign Office remained an important stepping-stone, but the Home Office was replaced by the Exchequer. . .

This brings me to a final question. How different were the actual policies of the two men, as opposed to their political styles and public images? The perspective of history tends to diminish political differences. We can see now that their basic views on the monarchy,

THE CHOICE OF HERCULES.

F 'Alternative Paths'

the rights of property, the importance of landed estates, the enlargement of the electorate did not differ so very greatly. Both would have repudiated the levelling trends of the twentieth century. Gladstone declared that he was 'an out and out inequalitarian'. So was Disraeli. Both were opposed to the extension of the sphere of government, and both would have been horrified by its features today. Yet, when that is said, important divergencies remain. Gladstone believed intensely in nationalism, in the virtues of 'nations struggling rightly to be free'. He sensed the 'wind of change' in Ireland long before anyone else of his calibre and status. He combined this with a deep conviction that political action should be a moral crusade, and that the great issues were essentially moral issues transcending particular British interests. He believed in the comity of nations, the concert of Europe, obedience to international law, the acceptance of arbitration. His attitude, with its idealism, its contradictions, its dilemmas, has coloured the parties of the left to some extent ever since.

Disraeli repudiated all this. The only nationalism with which he sympathised was English nationalism. This was in no way incompatible with being singularly un-English himself. All other nationalisms he suspected or ignored. Politics to him was not a question of high morality or crusading zeal. It was a matter of practical problems to be solved by commonsense and a proper assertion of English interests. He believed in Realpolitik and the use of power. This was why he got on so well with Bismarck. His language may have been high flown, extravagant, fantastic, but it clothed a Palmerstonian attitude of straight English patriotism, no-nonsense with foreigners, and preservation of the Empire. His attitude, with its dilemmas and difficulties, has to some extent coloured that of the right ever since.

from 'Disraeli and Gladstone', the 1969 Leslie Stephen Lecture
by Lord Blake

Questions

1 What does Philip Magnus (Source A) identify as Gladstone's major contributions to British politics? **(9 marks)**

2 Examine the significance of the following references in Source B:
   (a) 'Gladstone's new position with the electorate' (lines 14–15)
   (4 marks)
   (b) 'he made astute use of the growth of the newspaper press' (line 26) **(4 marks)**

(*c*) 'Gladstone combined an exact attention to publicity with a most
advantageous appearance of unworldliness' (lines 37–38)

(4 marks)

3 In Source C, how does H C G Matthew substantiate his claim that
'Gladstone's career displays the strengths and weaknesses of a
Liberal democracy' (lines 25–26)? **(7 marks)**

4 In Source D, what does Richard Shannon regard as the chief
differences in political attitude between Disraeli and Gladstone?

(9 marks)

5 How closely do Sources D and E concur in their assessments of
Disraeli and Gladstone? **(9 marks)**

11 DEALING WITH EXAMINATION QUESTIONS

Specimen Answers to Source-based Questions

Questions based on Chapter 4 – 'Disraeli and Conservatism' (See pages 39–49)

Questions

1 Explain the meaning of the following terms as they appear in Source D:
  (*a*) 'hereditary coteries of exclusive nobles' (line 4) **(2 marks)**
  (*b*) 'my Lord Derby and his colleagues have taken a happy opportunity
     to enlarge the privileges of the people of England' (lines 9–10)
     (2 marks)

2 Using your own knowledge, examine the political significance of the fears
   expressed by Salisbury in Source G. **(7 marks)**

3 In Sources D and H, Disraeli frequently uses the phrase 'the institutions
   of the country'. What did he mean by this? **(7 marks)**

4 How far can an understanding of Disraeli's Conservatism be drawn from
   Sources D and H? **(8 marks)**

5 How valuable to the historian is the analysis in Document I of the 1874
   election results? **(9 marks)**

Points to note about these questions

1 (*a*) 'Explain' here means to put into your own words.
  (*b*) 'Explain' here means that you have to describe *briefly* what Derby and
     the Conservatives had recently done in regard to the Second Reform
     Bill. This calls on your own knowledge of the background.

2 This is asking you to explain Salisbury's doubts regarding Disraeli's
   leadership. This can be done adequately by paraphrasing what Salisbury
   says in his letter, but an even better answer is to add from your own
   knowledge points explaining why he is so worried. In examining the political
   significance of his fears, you need to say how the attitude of Conservatives
   like Salisbury affected Disraeli's position as leader of the Party.

3 To answer this well, you would need to call on your prior knowledge as
   well as the evidence in the extract. Examiners expect candidates to be able
   to explain important terms like 'institutions'.

4 This calls for careful analysis of what Disraeli says in Sources D and H. The answer can be drawn solely from the extracts but to give a high quality response to the 'How far' part of the question it is necessary to put his statements in the wider context of his career.

5 This question requires you to assess the value to the historian of Harrison's interpretation. It is vital, therefore, that you convey your understanding of his description of the class support that Disraeli had won for the Conservative Party by 1874.

SPECIMEN ANSWERS

1 Explain the meaning of the following terms as they appear in Source D:
(*a*) hereditary coteries of exclusive nobles' (line 4) **(2 marks)**

Disraeli does not consider that the Tory Party is any longer simply a privileged group of landed magnates, wielding power by right of birth and responsible to no one but themselves.

(*b*) 'my Lord Derby and his colleagues have taken a happy opportunity to enlarge the privileges of the people of England' (line 9) **(2 marks)**

Here Disraeli is referring to the recent Reform Act of 1867, introduced by the Conservatives under Lord Derby, which increased the electorate by nearly a million and enfranchised a large proportion of working-class men.

2 Using your own knowledge, examine the political significance of the fears expressed by Salisbury in Source G. **(7 marks)**

Disraeli's opportunism in regard to the passing of 1867 Reform Bill had proved successful on two counts: it had stolen the thunder of the Liberals and it had greatly enhanced his position in the Conservative Party. This had dismayed Salisbury who belonged to that group of Conservatives who regarded Disraeli as an upstart. Concerned that the Party seems bent on promoting Disraeli's personal power, Salisbury observes that he lacks both birth and property and is, moreover, a dishonest and unprincipled adventurer. Salisbury laments the personal grip that Disraeli has begun to establish over the Conservatives. No one in the Cabinet appeared to have been willing to challenge him in regard to his forcing through of the Reform Bill. Disraeli's radicalism has been made still more dangerous by the attraction he holds for the disaffected Liberals who are now gravitating towards the Conservative Party because they believe their brand of radicalism is better represented by the irresponsible and unscrupulous Disraeli.

Salisbury's bitterness is an interesting example of the chronic distrust that many Conservatives felt towards Disraeli, something that was to dog him throughout his career.

3 In Sources D and H, Disraeli frequently uses the phrase 'the institutions of the country'. What did he mean by this? **(3 marks)**

The Established Church, which provided a framework of moral reference; the House of Lords, which expressed the virtues of the hereditary principle; the authority of the JPs in the counties, which guaranteed the rule of law; above all, the Crown, which symbolised the nation's identity: these were the English institutions that Disraeli revered.

4 How far can an understanding of Disraeli's Conservatism be drawn from Sources D and H? **(7 marks)**

In Source D, Disraeli points out how the Conservative Party had, by the introduction of the 1867 Reform Bill, both enlarged the rights of the English people and strengthened the institutions of the country. This, indeed, formed the basis of what came to be termed Tory Democracy.

It was in his celebrated Crystal Palace speech, Source H, that Disraeli first made his great appeal to Imperialism as an expression of national prestige and as a commitment in Conservative policy. Denouncing Liberal attempts over forty years to reduce Britain's status as an overseas and imperial power he pledged his Party to the restoration and enlargement of the Empire. Of equal weight in Conservative policy, as Disraeli put it in this speech, was the commitment to 'the elevation of the condition of the people'; this promise of social reform was a calculated appeal to the newly-enfranchised working-class voter. Interestingly, these two aspects of policy were interlocking; imperialism was to prove as attractive as social reform to the bulk of the working class in the last quarter of the century.

5 How valuable to the historian is the analysis in Document I of the 1874 election results? **(9 marks)**

It is observable in English politics that success is as often a matter of what is opposed as of what is proposed. Disraeli's breakthrough as a popular politican came with Gladstone's great reforming ministry of 1868–74. Scarcely any major institution was left untouched and while, by later standards, the reforms were barely dramatic, to contemporaries they seemed far-reaching and even ominous. The landed and the industrial classes became fearful. Disraeli played upon these fears with considerable skill, representing Gladstone and the Liberal Government as being hell-bent on the destruction of English institutions. As his speeches quoted in these Sources illustrate, Disraeli aimed to project an image of himself and the Conservative Party as bastions of reason, around whom men of moderation could rally in defence of national interests.

The success of such campaigning is depicted in Source I. The historian is able to appreciate how percipient Frederic Harrison was in highlighting this feature of Disraeli's Conservatism. Harrison had grasped that the shift of support by the middle classes to the Conservatives marked an important trend in English politics; the wider the franchise, the greater the necessity for parties to capture the middle ground, the vital territory in the battle for political support. Disraeli's understanding of the need to win over the middle classes was an essential ingredient in his Conservatism. His success in this respect guaranteed his Party an enduring place in English politics and government.

Key points to note in the answers

1 (*a*) This answer concentrates on defining the quoted term as a description of the old Tory Party. Note that as only two marks are allocated to this part of the question the answer has to be very much to the point.
  (*b*) Again, precision is called for in a two-mark answer. Notice how the answer stresses the Reform Act of 1867 as the key factor.

2 Note how this answer combines analysis of the document with important background material. Political significance is emphasised in the second part of the answer.

3 Observe how this answer goes straight to the point and clearly defines what Disraeli understood by 'institutions'; namely, Church, Lords, JPs, and monarchy. This calls on prior knowledge.

4 A more difficult question, this; note how the answer uses both the evidence in the two speeches and a wider knowledge of Disraeli's Conservatism. This is the safest way to tackle a 'how far' type of question.

5 The emphasis here is on the quality of Harrison's insights into the nature of the middle-class support for Disraeli's Conservatism. The views of this informed contemporary are of considerable value to the modern historian.

Preparing Essay Answers

Contrary to popular belief, examiners do not enjoy failing candidates. The problems are largely made in the examination room by the candidates themselves. As the reports of the examination boards point out year after year, the greatest single weakness among examinees is an inability to be relevant in their answers. No matter how well read and knowledgeable candidates may be, if they stray too far from the terms of the question they cannot be given credit. Examinations from 'A' level upwards are basically a test of the candidates' ability to analyse historical material in such a manner as to present a reasoned, informed, response to a specific question. Too often examiners are faced with regurgitated notes on a set of topics, little of which relates to the questions as set. There really is no such animal as an 'easy' exam question at these levels; those who set the papers seldom repeat the exact wording of their questions. This means that each question demands its own individual interpretation. The intelligence and subtlety of the candidates' response will determine how high a mark they score. Examinees must, of course, have 'knowledge', but academic history tests not only *what* they know but how well they *use* what they know.

As an aid to the development of effective examination technique, here is a list of questions that candidates should ask themselves when preparing their essays:

1 *Have I answered the question as SET* or have I simply imposed my prepared answer on it? (It is remarkable how many exam scripts contain answers to questions that do not appear on the exam paper!)

2 *Have I produced a genuine argument* or have I merely put down a number of disconnected points in the hope that the examiners can work it out for themselves? (Too many answers consist of a list of facts rounded off by the 'Thus it can be seen. . .' type of statement which seldom relates to what has been previously written.)

3 *Have I been relevant in arguing my case* or have I included ideas and facts that have no real relation to the question? (Some candidates simply write down all they know about a topic, assuming that sheer volume will overwhelm the examiner into giving a satisfactory mark. This 'mud-at-the-wall' method is counter-productive since it glaringly exposes the candidate's inability to be selective or show judgement.

4 *Have I made appropriate use of primary or secondary sources to illustrate my answer?* (Examiners do look for evidence of intelligent reading. Choice, apt, quotation from documents or books does elevate the quality of an answer. Acquaintance with the ideas of modern historians and authorities is a hallmark of the better prepared candidate. However, discretion needs to be shown; putting in quotations where they are not relevant or inserting over-long, rote-learned passages merely looks like padding.)

5 *Have I tried to show originality* or have I just played safe and written a dull, uninspired answer? (Remember, examiners have to plough through vast quantities of dreary, ill-digested material from large numbers of candidates. When, therefore, they come across a script that shows initiative and zest, their interest and sympathy are engaged. A candidate who applies his own reasoning and interpretation to a question may occasionally make naive statements but, given that his basic understanding and knowledge are sound, his ambition will be rewarded. This is not an encouragement to 'waffle' but it is to suggest that, provided always that he keeps to the terms of the question, the candidate is free to follow his own judgements. A thought-provoking answer is likely to be a good answer.)

One final, cautionary, word: never try to be funny in an answer. Humour is like a delicate wine; it does not always travel well. What the candidate thinks is rib-splittingly hilarious may well leave his reader cold. Examiners, like Queen Victoria, are not amused.

Possible Essay Titles

1 Consider the view that the 1867 Reform Act was a victory not for radicalism but for conservatism.

The question is asking whether the Act was a major extension of the franchise, in keeping with radical hopes, or a limited one, satisfying conservative instincts. Whatever line is taken, it is important that enough details of the Act be stated to substantiate the argument. There are certain key points worth stressing: the extension of the franchise was less important than the redistribution of seats; it was the latter that left the Conservatives still in command, since they retained the more numerous county seats. Liberal votes tended to pile up wastefully in the boroughs. No workingmen were returned to Parliament in the 1868 election. Disraeli saw the 1867 Act as offering the Conservative party definite electoral advantages.

2 How appropriate is the description of Gladstone's First Ministry as 'the hightide of Liberalism'?

'Liberalism' here calls for some definition. If it is interpreted as 'peace, retrenchment and reform', there is a good case for saying that 1868–74 marks a high point. However, it could also be said that legislative success is not necessarily the same as political success; the fact that the reforms offended so many vested interests proved damaging to the Liberal Party. A further consideration is that since it is impossible to detach Liberalism from Gladstone it might be more reasonable to claim that Liberalism was at its height later when Gladstone fought his great moral campaigns over the Eastern Question and Ireland.

3 Was Disraeli an indispensable liability to the Conservative Party?

This is asking for an analysis of why Disraeli was regarded both as a saviour and a danger to the party he led. It has to do with his being seen as a radical upstart by the traditional Tory elements, who at the same time could not deny that his particular political gifts were a major electoral asset. The lack of a serious challenger to his eminence in the party meant the Tories were stuck with him. Reference to Robert Blake, who coined the term in question, would be appropriate; his emphasis on Disraeli as the creator of a Conservatism that, by appealing across the classes, guaranteed the Party's survival as a political force could well furnish the basis of the answer.

4 What were the essentials of Gladstonian Liberalism?

This is not perhaps as straightforward as it appears. It is asking for a considered selection from the many aspects of Gladstone's activities of those features which were integral to his Liberalism. It could be argued that these were not fixed but changed as his career developed. An important distinction could usefully be drawn between the Liberal party as a political movement and Liberalism as an expression of Gladstone's deep commitment to what he regarded as the great moral causes of his time. It is arguable that Gladstone was less interested in the former than the latter, and that the essentials of his Liberalism can be determined more positively by studying his involvement in such issues as Italy, the Eastern Question and Ireland.

5 How consistent were Disraeli's imperial policies?

This question is obviously seeking an explanation for Disraeli's sudden adoption of imperialism as a major part of his Conservatism. Having been uninterested in colonies, Disraeli came to view British territorial interests overseas as of paramount importance. His imperialism was very much an affair of the 1870s and seems to have been prompted by the realisation that it could well prove a vote winner among the newly-enlarged electorate. It is not unreasonable to argue that once he had decided on an imperial approach he remained a model of consistency. This can be substantiated by an analysis of the four key areas of activity: the Royal Titles Bill, Suez, Afghanistan and South Africa.

6 Was it bad luck or bad judgement that prevented Gladstone from achieving Home Rule for Ireland?

It is significant that in his later reflections Gladstone attributed his failure over Home Rule to bad luck. He claimed that had the Parnell divorce scandal not weakened the Irish party at a critical moment in the 1890s then the Lords would never have had the pretext for opposing the measure. Equally, it could be claimed that there had been earlier misfortunes, such as the 'Hawarden kite', for which he was not responsible that had made his task unduly difficult. Against that may be set the thought that Gladstone frequently underestimated the strength and nature of the opposition to him over Ireland, which resulted in his adopting policies which were essentially unrealistic. It is necessary, therefore, to assess whether his judgement was at fault in expecting that in the circumstances of his time his Home Rule policy ever stood a genuine chance of being accepted.

7 'Expediency not principle dictated Disraeli's policy towards Turkey after 1875.' Discuss.

It might be argued that expediency and principle are not always in opposition. For example, Disraeli could be described as having, by his lights, a principled approach to the Eastern Question, namely, the preservation at all times of

British interests. Accordingly, his pro-Turkish sympathies and lack of concern for the plight of Turkey's Christian subjects were of a piece with his desire to defend Britain's concerns in the Near East. Conversely, it might be suggested that such an unbudging British stance almost ranks as a definition of expediency, since it denied Disraeli any opportunity of judging the Russo-Turkey issue on its merits. Whatever developments occurred, he was bound to an anti-Russian response.

Both sides of this argument should be put.

8 'Regarding the Eastern Question in 1876, Gladstone did not create the national mood, he responded to it.' Discuss.

This may appear to be a specialist question, but it relates to a vital aspect of Gladstone's celebrated involvement in the agitation over the Bulgarian atrocities. Knowledge of the work of Richard Shannon in this field would be of considerable advantage. Shannon's researches have shown that a well-organised campaign in Britain against the Turkish atrocities already existed in Britain before Gladstone entered the fray. What Gladstone did in 1876 was to seize a golden opportunity to make up for his defeat at Disraeli's hands two years earlier. He took the high moral ground from which to launch an attack upon the evils of Beaconsfieldism, an attack he sustained until his eventual victory over Disraeli in 1880. Gladstone's onslaught on the Turks was thus a mixture of genuine moral affront and political opportunism.

9 Why were Gladstone's last three administrations less successful than his first?

There are two key aspects: Gladstone's own attitudes, and the pressures to which he and the Liberal Party were subject in the second half of the century. Gladstone's 1868–74 ministry was the climax of the first stage of his career. It could be argued that this government exhausted the Liberal Party's legislative and reforming aims. It had gone as far as it could go. Hence during the last three ministries the reform programme was much less impressive. When Gladstone came out of retirement in 1876, he committed himself to the great causes of the Eastern Question and Ireland; these overshadowed domestic politics and distracted his Party from attending to the bread and butter questions of the day. This in turn led to a growing three-way division within the Party between Gladstone's followers, the Whigs who were offended by his Home Rule policy, and the Chamberlainite radicals who demanded that the Party concern itself with the pressing social issues of the day. Gladstone was also dragged, against his will, into foreign entanglements, eg Egypt, which brought his government little credit or popularity. In addition, the last three of Gladstone's governments seldom had a comfortable majority on which they could rely in the Commons.

10 'In the final analysis what Gladstone and Disraeli did was less important than what they were.' Discuss.

This quotation is suggesting that the significance of the two statesmen is in what they represented rather than in the work they performed. One response might be to say that this is a false opposition, that what they were was a product of what they did, or that what they did made them what they were. However, there is little doubt that Gladstone and Disraeli came respectively to personify Liberalism and Conservatism. Their personalities and abilities were such that they became indispensable to their parties. Yet this would not have mattered if their activities had not had an enduring effect upon the development of British politics and society. Between them they were responsible for a wide range of measures that began the process of adapting British institutions to the demands of industrial society. It is arguable that in the process, Disraeli restructured Conservatism as a modern political party, while Gladstone committed Liberalism to a programme that proved ultimately self-destructive.

Specimen Essay Answer

(*See pages 81–84*)

Trace and explain the stages by which Gladstone became converted to the principle of Home Rule for Ireland.

Believing that it was his 'mission to pacify Ireland' and bring it to a state of 'national content', Gladstone set out in 1868 on a deliberate policy of corrective legislation that would end Irish grievances. This commitment was to dominate the remainder of his political life down to 1894. Whatever the success of his individual measures in regard to religion, the land and education (the so-called Upas Tree of Irish problems), the Irish question itself had manifestly not been solved by the time of his second administration in 1880; outrages and repression had increased in severity. Through historical study and abstract reasoning (he had no direct experience of Ireland) Gladstone had moved by 1883 to a position where he considered that the control of Ireland by 'the present highly centralised system of Government' was the fundamental reason for Irish bitterness. Local issues, Gladstone felt, must be dealt with locally. He remarked that only when 'a popular and responsible *Irish* body' was installed could there be peace.

This was not yet an argument for separation from England, but it did suggest that Ireland must be allowed a large measure of self-government over matters of immediate concern to herself. Gladstone's mind in the early 1880s began to move step by step towards the Home Rule principle to which he would openly admit being converted in 1886. By a process of logic, Gladstone came to appreciate that Ireland was not a single question but was composed

119

of a number of inter-locking grievances and ills, economic, religious, social and political. This amalgam of problems heightened Irish nationalism and made the solution of the Irish question impossible merely by means of righting a series of wrongs. It was the realisation of this that led him towards the possibility of Anglo-Irish separation. He believed that a separate Irish legislature could work harmoniously in conjunction with the rule of the Westminster government. History told him that it had, indeed, done so before the Act of Union in 1800, and he calculated that it could do so again.

He became so certain that this was the just solution that he was quite prepared to co-operate with the Conservatives in a bi-partisan introduction of some form of Home Rule or even to support a Conservative government implementing the measure as its own. However, when the Conservatives learned through 'the Hawarden kite', an unintentional revelation by Gladstone's son, Herbert, of his father's conversion to Home Rule, the Conservatives were only too willing to hand the 'poisoned chalice' back to Gladstone. Aware that neither the Hartington Whigs nor the Chamberlainite radicals would accept Home Rule, Gladstone nonetheless persevered, even at the risk of splitting the Liberal Party. This duly happened. In 1886, his first Home Rule Bill was defeated on its second reading in the Commons as a result of some ninety Liberals joining with the Conservatives in voting against it.

BIBLIOGRAPHY

There are hundreds of books dealing with these two outstanding statesmen and their times. The following list is intended as a guide to some of the most accessible and readable studies.

Paul Adelman: *Gladstone, Disraeli and Later Victorian Politics* (Longman 1970). A clear, concise, treatment of the major themes – contains a helpful set of documents and an excellent bibliography.

Robert Blake: *The Conservative Party from Peel to Churchill* (Eyre & Spottiswood 1970 – also in Fontana Paperback). Contains important sections dealing with the growth of the Conservative Party under Disraeli.

Robert Blake: *Disraeli* (Eyre & Spottiswood 1966). Generally recognised as one of the great biographies of our time – contains fascinating insights into Disraeli as a politician, a writer and a man; long but not too long.

Maurice Cowling: *1867 Disraeli, Gladstone and Revolution* (CUP 1967). An important analysis of the attitudes of Gladstone and Disraeli towards reform.

E J Feuchtwanger: *Gladstone* (Allen Lane 1976). A very readable study of Gladstone's development from politician to statesman.

Robin Grinter: *Disraeli and Conservatism* (Edward Arnold 1968). A booklet containing a useful selection of documents with linking commentary.

J L Hammond: *Gladstone and the Irish Nation* (first published in 1938, reprinted with an introduction by M R D Foot, Cass 1964). A detailed study which has become the reference point for all subsequent analyses of Gladstone's involvement with Ireland.

Peter J Jagger (ed): *Gladstone, Politics & Religion* (St Martin's Press 1985). An invaluable book, which contains a series of published lectures on Gladstone by such scholars as Lord Blake ('Disraeli and Gladstone'), M R D Foot ('The Gladstone Diaries'), Agatha Ramm ('Gladstone as Politician'), Owen Chadwick ('Young Gladstone and Italy'), Richard Shannon ('Midlothian: 100 Years After') and David Steele (Gladstone and Palmerston, 1855–65').

George Kitson Clark: *The Making of Victorian England* (Methuen 1962). One of those books that every genuine student of the period should read – it provides an invaluable introduction to the times in which Disraeli and Gladstone lived.

Philip Magnus: *Gladstone* (John Murray 1954). The first modern biography to make extensive use of Gladstone's papers – now an established modern classic.

H C G Matthew: *Gladstone 1809–74* (OUP 1988). This is the most up-to-date and informed study of Gladstone available, written by the leading authority on Gladstone and editor of the *Gladstone Diaries*.

Agatha Ramm: *William Ewart Gladstone* (University of Wales Press 1989). A short, stimulating, biography, that is particularly good on the Irish question.

Patrick Rooke: *Gladstone and Disraeli* (Wayland 1973). A simple but useful introduction, with an excellent set of visual illustrations.

L C B Seaman: *Victorian England* (Methuen 1973). A provocative study, providing a useful general background as well as some stimulating chapters on Gladstone and Disraeli.

Richard Shannon: *The Crisis of Imperialism, 1865–1915* (Hart-Davis 1974). A major modern work covering the critical years of the rivalry between Gladstone and Disraeli and assessing their significance as creative politicians.

John K Walton: *Disraeli* (Routledge 1990). One of the 'Lancaster Pamphlet' series – a short but very informative treatment of Disraeli as party leader, social reformer and imperialist.

INDEX